Golden Rules
for
Everyday Life

Translated from the French
Original title : RÈGLES D'OR POUR
LA VIE QUOTIDIENNE

Omraam Mikhaël Aïvanhov

Golden Rules
for
Everyday Life

4th edition
Second printing March 2000

Izvor Collection — No. 227

P R O S V E T A

Canadian Cataloguing in Publication Data

Aïvanhov, Omraam Mikhaël, 1900-1986
    Golden rules for everyday life

    (Izvor collection ; 227)
    Translation of: Règles d'or pour la vie quotidienne.
    ISBN 1-895978-17-3

    1. Conduct of life. I. Title. II. Series: Izvor collection
(North Hatley, Quebec) ; 227.

BJ1582.A3913 2000   170'.44   C00-900444-0

Prosveta Inc.
3950, Albert Mines, North Hatley, QC, Canada J0B 2C0

        Prosveta S.A. — B.P. 12 — 83601 Fréjus Cedex (France)

TABLE OF CONTENTS

1. Life : our most precious possession

So many people ruin their lives in their eagerness to acquire all kinds of possessions that are worth far less than life itself. Have you ever thought about this ? If you learned to give priority to life, if you took care to treasure and protect it and keep it in a state of perfect integrity and purity, you would have far more opportunity to fulfil all your wishes, for when life is enlightened, illuminated and intense it gives us all the rest.

You take life for granted and think that you are free to do whatever you like with it but, one day, after years spent in the pursuit of your own ambitions, you will be so exhausted and disillusioned that, if you weigh up all that you have gained against all that you have lost, you will find that you have lost almost everything and gained practically nothing. People say, 'Since I possess life, I can use it to get all the other things I want — money, pleasure, knowledge, glory etc.', and they draw heedlessly on their reserves until, one day, there is nothing left and they are obliged to give up all their activities. It is senseless to behave like that, for, in losing your life you lose everything. The essential thing is life itself, and you must protect, purify and strengthen it and reject whatever hampers or inhibits it, because it is thanks to life that you will obtain health, beauty, power, intelligence, love and true wealth.

Henceforth, therefore, work at embellishing, intensifying and sanctifying your life. You will soon feel the results, for a pure, harmonious life reverberates in other regions and touches a multitude of other entities and they will come to help and inspire you.

2. Let your material life be consistent with your spiritual life

Nobody asks you to imitate certain mystics and ascetics, who fled from the temptations and difficulties of the world, and to neglect your material life while dedicating yourself exclusively to prayer and meditation. On the other hand, more and more people today are totally absorbed by material concerns, and that is not the right solution, either.

Everyone should be in a position to work, earn a living and have their own family and, at the same time, possess the inner light and the methods they need to work at their own evolution.

You have to develop both the spiritual and the material aspects of your lives, to be in the world while, at the same time, living a Heavenly life. This is the goal you should aim for. It is difficult, to be sure, because you are still at the stage where, when you engage in spiritual activities, you let your material affairs go to pieces and, when you take care of your material affairs, you neglect your spiritual life. But you must have both. Both are necessary and both are possible. How ? Well, before undertaking anything, always say to yourself, 'My goal is to obtain true light, love and power : shall I get them by doing thus and so ?' Examine the situation carefully and, if you see that such or such an activity or interest deflects you from your ideal, abandon it.

3. Dedicate your life to a sublime goal

It is very important to know for whom and for what purpose you are working, because it is this that determines the orientation of your energies. If you dedicate yourself to a sublime ideal, your life will continually grow in richness, strength and intensity. It is like a capital investment : you place your capital in a Heavenly bank so that, instead of deteriorating or going to waste, it increases and makes you richer. And when you are richer you will be in a position to learn better and to work better. He who abandons himself to pleasures, emotions and passions squanders his capital — his life — because all those things have to be paid for, and he pays for them with his life. Whereas, if you invest your capital in a Heavenly bank, the more you work the stronger you become, because new, purer and more luminous elements continually pour into you to replace those you spend.

4. Our daily life : a matter that must be transformed by the spirit

You must learn to infuse into all your actions, into even the simplest things you do in your daily life, forces and elements that enable you to transpose them onto a spiritual plane and, in this way, to reach a higher level of life.

Take any ordinary day : as soon as you awake in the morning, a series of events — thoughts, feelings and actions — is set in motion. You get out of bed, switch on the light, open your windows, wash, get breakfast, go to work, meet other people, etc., etc. What a lot of things there are to do — and everbody has to do them. The only difference lies in the *way* they do them : some do them mechanically, automatically, but those who have a spiritual philosophy try to introduce a purer and more intense life into each action so that everything they do is transformed, everything takes on new meaning and they feel constantly inspired.

Of course, there are a lot of very dynamic, enterprising people in the world, but everything they do is designed to obtain success, money and glory ; they never do anything to give their lives greater serenity, balance or harmony. This is not intelligent of them, because all that feverish activity will only end by wearing them out and making them ill.

Get into the habit, therefore, of seeing your daily life, with all the little things you have to do every day, all the events that occur, all the people you meet and with whom you live, as a raw material which you are working to transform. Don't be content to accept everything as it comes, to resign yourself and be purely passive ; you must always add an element capable of animating, vivifying and spiritualizing this raw material. For this is what the spiritual life really is : the ability to infuse into everything you do this special element, this leaven that is capable of raising it to a higher plane. You will say, 'What about prayer and meditation ? Don't they come into it ?' Indeed they do : it is through prayer and meditation that you acquire the subtler, purer elements that enable you to give your activities this new dimension.

There may be times in your life when events make it impossible for you to practise the spiritual exercises that you are in the habit of practising, but this must not prevent you from being constantly in contact with the Spirit, for the Spirit transcends forms and practices. There is no situation or circumstance in which your life cannot be animated and made beautiful by your contact with the Spirit.

5. *Nutrition as Yoga*[1]

Many people, feeling that their sanity is threatened by their hectic way of life, take up yoga, Zen or Transcendental Meditation or various techniques of relaxation, hoping that they will help them to regain their balance. This is all well and good but I can give you a simpler and far more effective method : learn to eat correctly. What is so surprising in this ? Instead of eating carelessly and hurriedly, in the midst of noise, agitation and arguments and then going off to do yoga exercises, wouldn't it be much better to understand that meals give you the perfect opportunity every day, two or three times a day, to practise relaxation, concentration and the harmonization of all the cells of your body ?

1 See 'The Yoga of Nutrition', *Collection Izvor*, No. 204, which discusses this question at length.

When you sit down to a meal, begin by ridding your mind of anything that may prevent you from eating in peace and harmony. And if you don't succeed at once, wait until you are calm before beginning to eat. If you eat while you are upset, angry or irritable, that agitation and lack of harmony will affect your vibrations and communicate itself to everything you do. Even if you try to appear calm and in control, you will convey a sense of agitation and tension ; you will make mistakes, bump into the furniture or into other people and speak thoughtlessly, causing people to withdraw their friendship and doors to be closed to you. Whereas, if you are in a state of harmony when you eat, you will be better able to solve the problems that come your way and, even if you spend the rest of your day rushing from one activity to the next, you will be inhabited by a peace that nothing can destroy. Only if you begin at the beginning, with little things, will you be able to go on to much greater things.

Don't make the mistake of thinking that fatigue is always a result of overwork ; it is very often caused by a wasteful use of energy. And this applies here : when you swallow your food without chewing it properly and, particularly, without having impregnated it with your thoughts and feelings, it is less digestible and your organism will have difficulty in assimilating it and will not benefit from it as it should.

When you eat without being aware of the importance of what you are doing, your body is still strengthened by the food, to be sure, but it gets only the crudest and most material particles from it and this is nothing compared to the energies that you would receive if you really knew how to concentrate and eat in silence, for then you would extract all the etheric, subtle elements the food contains. During your meals, therefore, concentrate and project rays of love into your food so that the energy it contains is separated from the matter : when you do this, the matter disintegrates, whereas the energy is absorbed by your body and becomes available to you.

The important thing in nutrition is not the food itself but the energy, the quintessence it contains, for in this quintessence is life. The food-stuff itself is only a medium, and the pure, subtle quintessence it contains must not be used to nourish only the lower planes, the physical, astral and mental bodies ; it must also nourish the soul and spirit.

6. Respiration

'Chew' the air you breathe

Get into the habit of doing a few breathing exercises during the day and be sure to breathe slowly and deeply so that the practice is really beneficial. Give the fresh air time to fill your lungs and get down to the very bottom, so that it can replace the stale, impure air trapped in them. And not only must you draw slow, deep breaths, you must also hold your breath for a few seconds, from time to time, before breathing out again. Why ? In order to 'chew' it, for your lungs can 'chew' air just as the mouth chews food. The air we breathe in is like a mouthful of food loaded with life-giving energies but, if you want to get the most out of those energies, you have to give your lungs time to chew and digest it. When you do deep breathing exercises, therefore, try to be conscious that, with the air you are taking into your body, you are absorbing divine life.

The psychic and spiritual dimensions

Breathing exercises are good for our health, to be sure, but they are also good for our will and our mind. Try this experiment : when you have to lift something heavy, start by taking a deep breath and you will find that you can lift it more easily. In all the little details of everyday life, in your relations with others, remember to breathe deeply : it will help you to remain in control of yourself. Before an interview, for example, if you want to ensure that a discussion does not degenerate into a quarrel, get into the habit of taking a deep breath. And if you are feeling jumpy or upset, why not ask your lungs

to help you ? That is what they are there for.
Breathe deeply for two or three minutes and you
will find that you are quite calm again. It is normal to need help from time to time, but why do you
always have to look for it on the outside when it
is there, inside you ?

As you come to understand the deeper
significance of respiration, you will gradually feel
that your own breathing is beginning to blend into
that of the cosmos. As you breathe out, think that
you are expanding to the very outer limits of the
universe and then, as you breathe in again, you
contract and withdraw into yourself, into your ego,
that imperceptible point at the centre of an infinite
circle. Again you expand, and again you contract
…In this way you begin to discover the movement
of ebb and flow which is the key to all the rhythms
of the universe. When you become conscious of this
movement within your own being, you enter into
the harmony of the cosmos and establish a relationship of exchange between yourself and the universe,
for, as you breathe in, you inhale elements from
space and, as you breathe out, you send out into
space, something of your own heart and soul.
He who learns to be in harmony with the respiration of the cosmos enters into the sphere of divine
consciousness. Once you become really aware of
that dimension, you will want to spend your lives

working to inhale the strength and light of God so as to breathe out that light again to the whole world. For to breathe out is also to distribute to others the light of God that you have drawn into yourself.

Conscious breathing contains untold blessings for one's physical, emotional, intellectual and spiritual life. You should be able to see its beneficial effects on your brain as well as in your soul and in all your faculties ; it is a very powerful factor for every aspect of life. Never neglect the question of respiration[2].

7. *How to recuperate energy*

Too often, you let yourselves get caught up in the fevered atmosphere that is now a normal aspect of many people's lives and which is extremely detrimental to their psychic equilibrium. From now on, you must take better care of your nervous system and give it a chance to relax from time to time. For example, you can retire into a quiet room and stretch out face down on a bed, or flat on the floor, arms and legs relaxed. Let yourself go as though you were sinking into an ocean of light and remain motionless, without thinking of anything,

2 See the Brochure No.303, *Respiration ; spiritual dimensions and practical applications.*

for just one minute ! A minute or two later, when you stand up, your batteries will be recharged. There, that is all ; it is not much, but it is very important.

Of course, you will say that it is not always possible to stretch out in this way. That doesn't matter ; you can sit down, instead ; what does matter is to break the tenseness that has you in its grip. You must learn to relax, and not just once or twice a day ; that is not enough. You must do so ten, fifteen, twenty times a day. It need only be for a minute or two, but it is essential to get into the habit of doing it frequently. As soon as you have a moment to spare, wherever you may be, instead of fretting at being kept waiting, for instance, take advantage of the occasion to relax and recover your balance and you will be all the readier to go back to your activities with renewed energy.

8. *Love makes us tireless*

The great secret in sustaining a high quality of activity is to learn to work with love, for it is love that strengthens, vivifies and resuscitates. You cannot get good results from your work if you don't love it, if you see it as nothing more than a way of earning a living. To be sure, it will earn you some money, but you will gradually lose all your joy and enthusiasm and find yourself becoming irritable.

Even your general health will deteriorate. You can work for hours with love and not feel the least bit tired, but if you work, even if only for a few minutes, without love, in a spirit of anger and revolt, everything starts to seize up inside you and all your strength seeps away.

It is important to understand the power and efficacy of love. Whatever you do, do it with love ...or don't do it at all ! For anything you do without love only fatigues and poisons you, and you need not be surprised to find yourself drained and ill. People are always asking how they can become tireless : the secret is to love what you do, for it is love that awakens man's latent energies.

9. Technical progress
frees man for spiritual work

The fact that science and technology provide more and more appliances and products that make life easier for you is no reason to let yourself become slack. You should see all these improvements as so many opportunities to give more time to spiritual activities. This is the true significance of technical progress : to free human beings. Yes, but to free them for another kind of work. If your external, material work becomes less laborious and time-consuming it is so that you may devote more time to learning to master and spiritualize your inner matter and, in this way, become a beneficial influence on the whole world. With every effort, every exercise, life takes on a different colour, a different flavour. People who have everything they could possibly need on the material level are often so disillusioned that they never feel any joy, and this is because they have no inner activity, their life is without intensity. If they were enlightened they would continue to enjoy all their possessions but without ceasing their inner work. It is this work that gives a flavour to everything.

10. Furnishing your inner dwelling

You must learn to pay more attention to the possibilities of the inner dimension, for it is there, in your inner world, that you spend your life. You are not always looking at, listening to, touching or tasting things on the outside, but you are always with yourself, in your inner world, and you have never learned to make use of all its wealth. This is the world that belongs to you : wherever you go, you take it with you and you can always rely on it, whereas the outer world is always liable to disappoint you. You may think, for a moment, that you have hold of something external, but you soon find that there is nothing there : it has been taken from you or you have lost it. If you are looking for abundance and fulfilment you must realize that it is only within yourself that you will find them. You don't know yourself. You don't know how rich you are, how many treasures of knowledge and power God has put into you. It is time you made an effort to sense the presence of these riches and learn to use them.

Let me illustrate this : there are people who have furnished and decorated their house or flat so beautifully that they have no desire to leave it and go somewhere where they will have to put up with noise and dust and traffic jams. And then there are others, who live in a miserable slum and have none of life's commodities, and they seize every opportunity to go out (not that this is really the solution, but still ...). And now, let's interpret this : a spiritual man is one who has furnished his inner world with such care that nothing is missing. Poetry, colours, music, everything he needs is there and it is painful to him to have to 'go out' and abandon all that beauty. Whereas ordinary people, who have never done anything to make their inner dwelling fit to live in, are always eager to go out and amuse themselves elsewhere. As soon as they are left alone with themselves they are bored and miserable.

Think about this for a moment and judge for yourself which is the better situation. Isn't it more to your advantage to improve the place you never leave, the place in which you spend all your days and nights ? Why allow your inner world to go to wrack and ruin and become a slum with broken windows and cobwebs in every corner ? Henceforth, pay more attention to making everything within you more beautiful, richer and more harmonious ; in this way, not only will you feel much more comfortable within yourself but you will also be in a position to welcome visitors into your magnificent dwelling. Yes, the spirits of light will be delighted to come and visit you ; they may even decide to give you the benefit of their presence and stay with you permanently.

11. The outer world is a reflection of your inner world

You must realize that you can never find something outside yourself that you have not already found within. Even if you found something outwardly, if you had not already found it inwardly, you would pass it by without seeing it. The more love, wisdom and beauty you have found inwardly, the more you will discover them all round you. You think that you have not seen certain things because they were not there. No, they were certainly there, but you haven't seen them because you have not developed them sufficiently within yourself. Don't delude yourself : the outer world is simply a reflection of the inner world and this means that you will not find wealth, peace or happiness outwardly if you have never made the effort to find them inwardly.

12. Make sure of a good future by the way you live today

You are often anxious about the future and worry about possible accidents, illness or poverty, but why poison your existence by thinking of all the bad things that might happen ? We never know what the future holds, that's true, but the best way to avoid the disasters you fear is to try to live sensibly in the present. The future will be what you have made it in the present. It is today that is important. Just as the present is a consequence, a result of the past, the future will be a projection of the present. Everything hangs together ; past, present and future cannot be separated. The future will be built on the foundations you lay today and, of course, if those foundations are faulty, it is no good hoping for a very bright future. If they are solidly built, on the other hand, there will be no need to worry : with healthy roots you will get a strong trunk and healthy branches and fruits.

The past is past but it has given birth to the present, and the present contains the roots of the future. This means that you must build your future in advance by improving the present.

To do this, you must say to yourself, every day,
'Let me see, what have I said and done, today ?
What kind of thoughts and feelings have I had ?'
And if you have done something wrong, if you have
entertained bad thoughts and feelings, you must
realize that this puts you on the side of the forces
of darkness and that those forces will destroy your
future.

If you have lived badly during the day, you must
at least try, before going to sleep, to diminish the
evil effects by having better thoughts and making
up your mind to do better next day. Your good
thoughts will be like a swarm of bees that clean and
mend everything overnight so that you can start off
next morning in better conditions.

13. Live in the fullness of the present

Some people live constantly in the past, their
own past. They are prisoners of the few events they
have experienced in life and are incapable of moving
ahead. Others, on the contrary, live in the future,
but a phantasmal, illusory future conjured up by
their own imagination and which will never exist in
reality. It is good to revert to the past from time
to time, but only if you do so in order to recognize
your mistakes or the wisdom of your actions and
to learn from what you see. In this way, the past

becomes a treasure-house of experiences that can be used to live better in the present.

But, while learning from the past, it can also be useful to look ahead and picture the distant future that God envisages for men, and think of the splendour, the light in which mankind is destined to live, one day. To be sure, a lot of people think of the future, but what kind of future ? They think, 'In a few years I'll be married ; we'll have children — a whole brood of them — and a cosy little house ; and it will be good to sit in front of the house in the evening and smoke a pipe and watch the cows — or the trains — go by ! We'll breathe in a little dust and then we'll go in and have supper and drink a glass of wine together before going to bed.' What a splendid future ! Many of you will protest, 'But that's not at all what we are looking forward to !' I know ; you look forward to making a lot of money, to being successful in business, to covering yourselves in glory, to becoming a Cabinet minister or President, to having a pretty girl in your arms night and day ...But what is all that worth ? It's pitiful !

You must learn to see beyond this shabby future and look for new horizons, open your windows onto the infinite so as to see what the future of mankind will really be, how God envisages it, and anticipate it already in your daily life. Don't let the question of time bother you. Don't say, 'Yes, but I'll be dead

by then ; it won't happen in my time', for, in saying
that, you will be refusing all that is truly beautiful ; you will be refusing to understand the true
meaning of life.

The present must be a time of conscious,
enlightened action, drawing its wisdom from the
lessons of the past and stimulated by all the
possibilities of the future. This is the perfect situation : the lessons of the past (and, God knows,
mankind's past holds many lessons) and the infinite
possibilities of the future. If you know how to live
in the present in such a way as to express the experience of the past and the splendours of the future,
you will be close to the Godhead. What is it that
the Seraphim sing before the throne of God ? 'Holy,
holy, holy, Lord God Almighty, Who was and is
and is to come !' Your consciousness must expand
until it attains the dimensions of the divine
consciousness.

14. The importance of beginnings
Be aware of the forces you set in motion

You must never undertake anything until you
know what forces you will be setting in motion, for
it is the beginning that counts. It is at the moment
when something begins that certain forces are set
in motion, and these forces cannot be halted in mid-
flight ; they have to go all the way. Imagine, for

a moment, that you are up in the mountains and that a huge rock is just above you, precariously balanced on the edge of the precipice ; one little push would send it hurtling over the edge, and you are free to give it that push or to leave it alone. If you set it in motion it will be impossible to stop it : it will crush you and many others as well. Or suppose that you are standing by a dam : if you open the sluice gates, you will be powerless to stop the water from pouring out. It is always easy to set forces and events in motion but it is very difficult to steer them in the right direction and keep control of them. The term 'sorcerer's apprentice' applies to someone who rashly unleashes currents that he is incapable of controlling or orientating. It is easy for an agitator to start a riot but, once started, things can equally easily get out of hand and he loses control.

Before saying a word, giving someone a look, writing a letter or triggering an action, your power is absolute but, once events have been set in motion, you become a mere spectator and, often enough, a victim. This law is valid on the physical, astral and mental planes. If, when you feel yourself getting angry, you immediately decide to contain it, it will not burst from you but, if you let it explode, you will be unable to stop it running its course. And this is also true for certain ideas : if you let them take root in you, they will end by being ineradicable. Be watchful, therefore, and never forget that it is only at the beginning that you have any power.

Seek the light before acting

Before embarking on an enterprise of any importance, the first thing to do is to enter into yourself and make contact with the invisible world so as to ensure the best possible conditions for action. When someone is anxious and confused he is bound to make mistakes and complicate or even destroy things. In fact, it happens constantly : people act blindly and in haste, and the results are never satisfactory.

If you want to act correctly, you must first seek the light you need. Isn't this true, even on the purely physical plane ? Suppose that you are woken up in the middle of the night by a noise ; something has perhaps fallen over and broken, or a burglar has broken in to the house ...Would you rush off to investigate in the dark ? No ; you know that that would be dangerous. Before doing anything else you switch on the light. And, in every circumstance in life, the same rule applies : you must begin by switching on the light, that is to say, by turning inwards and concentrating so as to see what to do. If you don't have the light you need, you will waste time looking in different directions, knocking on all kinds of doors and trying all kinds of methods, and none of them will be effective.

Before undertaking anything important, therefore, you must concentrate for a few minutes on the world of light and ask for guidance. The response will come to you in the form of a particular idea or feeling or, possibly, in the form of a symbol. If the answer is perfectly clear, you can go ahead ; but if you are hesitant or apprehensive, or if something still seems unclear or contradictory, it means that there are obstacles or enemies in your way. In this case, postpone your decision, ask the same question the following day, and don't embark on your new venture until your way is clear and there are no further obstacles ahead.

Be careful about the first step

When you are about to do something for the first time, take care to be calm and to concentrate on accomplishing the very first gesture accurately and flawlessly. Then, do it again, a little faster. Keep practising, repeating it again and again, until you reach the right rhythm and speed, and you will see that it will become easier and easier and still be flawless. Whatever the gestures or actions you have to accomplish, you will always do so without a mistake if you take care to cut a perfect stereotype to start with.

If you constantly make mistakes in certain areas, it is because, without your realizing it, the first stereotypes you cut were flawed. If you were careless about the very first step, the first gesture, your initial contact with a person or an object, you will have made mistakes and now you are suffering the consequences ; as time goes on, those first mistakes have become graver and more numerous. It is very difficult to repair errors engraved in us in the past, but it is easy to learn how to make new, flawless stereotypes.

15. *Become conscious of your mental habits*

Human beings are rarely conscious of their own mental habits. When faced with a new task or a new situation, the immediate reaction of one person will be to become tense and irritable ; another will be pessimistic, critical or panic-stricken ; some will be violently opposed, others will be discouraged, and so on. But as none of them are aware of their attitudes, they are not in a position to remedy them and, in every circumstance, they will always find a pretext for reacting negatively. The first thing to do, therefore, is to study yourself and learn how you react. Once you see this clearly, you have the means you need to face up to every situation : it will give you the impetus to bring into play all the possibilities that God has implanted in your subconscious, your consciousness and your super-consciousness. In this way, thanks to your habit of looking at yourself with lucidity, you will be in a position to make constant progress.

16. Attention and vigilance

There are several different kinds of attention. The kind that is most familiar to us, of course, is the sustained mental application we have to use in order to do our work properly, listen to a lecture or read a book. But there is another kind of attention — call it self-observation or introspection, if you like — which consists of being aware, at every instant, of what is going on within oneself in order to recognize the currents, desires and thoughts that go through one. It is this kind of attention that is still not sufficiently developed. This is why, when you have a problem to solve or something important to understand, your brain is tired and clouded and you achieve nothing.

If your brain is to be constantly lucid and ready for work, you must be attentive, prudent, economical and moderate in all your activities, otherwise, even if Truth itself appeared before your eyes, you would still understand nothing. It is only by keeping your mental faculties constantly alert and on guard that you will be capable of dealing reasonably and intelligently with every situation as it arises.

A person who is not vigilant, who closes his eyes, is exposed to every possible danger. There is nothing worse than to go through life with one's eyes closed. You must keep your eyes open so as to know, at every instant, what your inner state of consciousness is. Only those who keep their eyes open possess the intelligence of the inner life and can no longer fall a prey to every alien force or entity. The thing is so obvious : someone who is asleep can always be taken by surprise !

From now on, therefore, remember this constant inner attention that will enable you to know exactly what is going on inside you. Of course, it takes practice, and a daily examination of conscience in the evening is not enough : at every moment of the day, you should be able to recognize the desires, thoughts and feelings that fill your mind, know their true nature and where they come from and, if necessary, arm yourself against them or repair any damage they may have done.

When a disaster occurs in the ordinary way of life, we see how firemen or soldiers immediately come to the rescue to put out a fire, repair bridges, clear the roads, rescue the injured and so on. People find it perfectly natural to repair physical damage immediately but, when it comes to the inner world, they don't know what to do ; they look on without reacting as the destruction continues. No ; you must look into yourself and see what needs to be repaired, five, ten, twenty times a day, and not leave it until later. Otherwise, when 'later' comes, it will be too late ; you will have already fallen to pieces and been wiped out.

17. Stick to one spiritual path

If you want to do any serious spiritual work you must stick to one philosophy, one system, and go into it in depth, for the psychic organism reacts in exactly the same way as the physical organism : if you make it swallow too many different kinds of food it gets indigestion and falls ill. What can you possibly do with a hotchpotch of Egyptian, Hindu, Tibetan, African, Chinese, Hebrew and Aztec traditions ? It is not as though your mental structure were strong enough to know how to navigate in the midst of all that. Many of you are barely able to form a clear idea of a single philosophical system, so what can you hope to gain by reading and studying everything ? It can only go to your head. And then, of course, everybody says that it is spirituality that drives people out of their mind. But it is not the fault of spirituality if people insist on treating it like a fair in which they can sample all kinds of exotic attractions, even such dangerous attractions as drugs, black magic and unbridled sexuality. It is time you understood that true spirituality means that you yourself become the

living expression of the divine Teaching you
follow.

18. Practice is more important than theory

Try to grasp the fundamental difference between
spiritual and intellectual work. Let's say that I give
you an orange : your intellect enables you to acquire
a lot of information about that orange : its shape
and weight and colour, where and when it was
grown, its particular properties and the chemical
elements it contains, the different ways it can be used and, even, its symbolic significance. In an Initiatic school you will learn none of that, but you
will learn the one thing that is essential : you will
learn to taste it. This is what spiritual work is : not
to store up masses of theoretical information but
to 'eat', to taste, the orange ; that is to say, to gain
practical experience, applied knowledge. This is
more difficult than theoretical knowledge ; it requires an effort, but it is the only way to transform
oneself.

Of course, no one can deny that it is interesting
and, even, useful to learn about the attempts that
human beings have been making for hundreds and
thousands of years to pierce the mysteries of the
universe and approach the Godhead, but it is not
enough. Since the one concern of all these religions
and philosophical systems is the splendour, the

divinization, the perfecting of man, we must make an effort to achieve that ideal. Don't imitate the ridiculous behaviour of those who flock to highbrow lectures about the wisdom and science of the Initiates of the past, without realizing how small, petty and weak they are and how incapable of giving a reasonable direction to their own lives. That is not spirituality.

19. Moral qualities are more valuable than talent

Everybody admires the man or woman who manifests an outstanding talent for art, science or sport ; they are not interested in knowing whether he or she is kind, just, honest or generous : talent is the only thing that people really appreciate and try to cultivate. This is why the world today is full of people who are remarkably gifted and talented. But why are all these gifts and talents and skills unable to save the world ? Because that is not what is needed. If Providence has given you the talent to be a poet, musician, physicist, economist or swimming champion and you have cultivated that talent, that is magnificent, but what really matters is to live according to the divine laws ; that is to say, to work, every day of your life, to acquire greater wisdom, greater integrity and generosity and greater self-mastery. The world needs people who are capable of manifesting moral qualities far more than it needs artists, scientists, athletes, etc. Take care, therefore, not to let yourself be too impressed by gifted, talented people, and never make it your ideal to be like them. Your ideal must be the highest possible : to come a little closer to perfection every day. And perfection is to be like the sun, luminous, warm and vivifying, so as to awaken, enlighten, stimulate and fecundate all creatures.

20. Be contented with your lot and discontented with yourself

There are different ways of being contented. The first way is that of animals : they are satisfied with their lot, because they have no perception of their limitations and no reason to try to progress beyond them. This mentality is normal for animals, but it is not good for human beings although, in fact, many of them are quite satisfied with it. Another way of being content with one's lot is what we might call 'acceptance' : a person understands that the trials he has to endure are the consequence of his past errors, so he puts up with them. But he does not stop there : he knows that he has to make an effort to atone for his mistakes and make good his deficiencies. And this is the way of wisdom : to accept one's lot as the consequence of faults committed in previous incarnations but never to be satisfied with one's present degree of evolution, always to strive to make progress.

A sentiment of dissatisfaction with yourself, therefore, can be a stimulus that drives you to do better. But there must be another element to counterbalance this dissatisfaction, otherwise it can become a destructive obsession, and that element is your satisfaction with others. It is this that will save you from being too negative and giving way to discouragement. Look for the good and the beauty in all human beings, particularly in those who have contributed, by their genius and their virtues, to the evolution of mankind. In this way you will always have something to admire and be in no danger of falling into despair.

21. Spiritual work is never wasted

Nothing is more important or more salutary than to develop a taste and a love for spiritual activities and never to allow a single day to go by without meditating and praying and renewing your contact with Heaven. Pause for a few minutes, several times a day, to get in touch with your central core, that divine centre within. In this way, you will begin to sense that, whatever your outer circumstances, you possess an eternal, immortal indestructible element within you. Even though none of this can be seen, even if no one appreciates your efforts, even if you

get no material benefit from it, never cease to amass
a fortune in spiritual riches and you will become
so much freer and stronger inwardly that you will
be above all contingencies. This spiritual work is
your only wealth, the only thing that can truly be
said to belong to you. All the rest can be taken from
you ; only your work will be yours for ever.

22. The regeneration
of our physical, astral and mental bodies

Every thought, every feeling, every sentiment
and every one of our actions has the property of
attracting from space the material elements that correspond to it. Luminous, disinterested thoughts,
feelings, desires and actions that are upheld by a
firm intention of the will, attract particles of pure,
incorruptible matter. If, by the quality of your
psychic life, you work every day to attract these pure
particles, they will enter and take root in every part
of your organism and make themselves so much at
home that they will drive out all the old particles
of dusty, mouldy, shabby matter. In this way, little
by little, you will renew and regenerate your
physical, astral and mental bodies.

By contemplating the manifestations of the
divine world in the form of light, beauty, music and
harmony, you receive a few of these new particles
and, as each particle is alive, it is never alone : it

brings with it corresponding forces and spirits. Your task, therefore, is to work, every day, to replace your old, worn out particles with new, Heavenly, radiant particles.

Someone might say, 'Why go to so much trouble to get results that will only last one lifetime ? Is it really worth it ?' Indeed it is, for, in reality, this is the only work that gives lasting results. When you leave this earth, the only fortune you can take with you will be the inner treasures that you have acquired by your own efforts. And, when you come back for your next incarnation, you will bring these treasures back with you : from the moment of conception, during the period of gestation, the matter of your physical, astral and mental bodies will be fashioned and moulded to conform exactly with the qualities and virtues that you are developing today, in your present incarnation.

23. Look for some spiritual food every day

In the morning, when you are looking at the sun, be aware that the rays that reach you are living beings that can help you to solve today's problems — but only today's, not tomorrow's. Tomorrow, you will have to go and ask for their help and advice again and, here too, only for one day. They will never answer you two or three days in advance. They will say, 'Don't fret. Come back tomorrow and we'll give you our answer then.' When you eat, you don't try to put enough food for a week into your stomach, only enough for one day. Today, you eat for today and, tomorrow, you begin all over again. And this is how it must be with light, for light is a food that you must absorb and digest every day so that it may become feelings, thoughts and inspirations within you.

Why don't we use the same logic in our approach to light as in our approach to food ? We say, 'Yes, I know that I ate yesterday, but that doesn't count any longer ; I need to eat again today.' And the same is true of light : we need to be nourished by light every single day.

24. *Periodically review your life*

It can be very beneficial to your development to get into the habit of periodically reviewing your life. Why ? Because, only too often, all the activities and cares that you have to contend with tend to give a direction to your life that takes you further and further from your spiritual ideal. You begin to forget that you will not be on this earth for long and that you are going to have to leave behind all your material possessions, your social rank and all those honorary titles that you have been at such pains to acquire. You will say that everybody knows that. True, everybody knows it but everybody forgets it ; and you, too : you get led away by the example of those around you. This is why it is indispensable to pause, from time to time, and to look back over your life and analyse the direction it has taken and the activities that absorb your time and attention. Each time you do this, you must sift things out and retain only what is essential.

25. *Choosing the means to fit the end*

One of the reasons why you don't make progress in your spiritual life is that you indulge in all kinds of activities that have no connection with your spiritual work, in the belief that they will not turn you away from the heights that you are aiming for. The truth is that, if you yield to the temptation to experience this and try that, regardless of the nature and quality of these experiments, when you want to rise to a higher level inwardly, you will find that you are unable to free yourself. If you cultivate a very elevated spiritual ideal, it necessarily involves depriving yourself of a few things. If you spend the night in all kinds of amusements and effervescence, do you think that you will be in a frame of mind conducive to meditation next morning ?

If some of you never make any progress, in spite of all the explanations and methods that you continually receive, it is because you still have too many interests and activities that are alien to the spiritual life : money, comfort, pleasure, social standing, etc. I am not saying that you have to do away completely with all these concerns or that they are absolutely incompatible with the spiritual life, but there is a question that needs to be sorted out first, and that is the question of the means and the end. Look at all the faculties that human beings possess and ask yourself what they use them for. What end do they serve ? The gratification of their sexual needs, their belly, their passions. Well, henceforth, you must do just the opposite, you must put all your faculties at the service of a high ideal, at the service of the spirit and of light.

Analyse yourselves and you will see how many of your divine gifts are being sacrificed to the whims of your lower nature. And then you complain, 'I'm all confused. I don't know where I am !' What can you expect ? When you accumulate an assortment of too many different elements, it is only normal to find yourself swamped in contradictions.

Take the example of a diamond : if a diamond is so extraordinarily pure, it is because there is no mixture in it : it is pure carbon. Add just one element to it and it would no longer be a diamond. Disciples who want to touch, taste, experiment and know about everything, lose their value as diamonds , they become ordinary, opaque stones. A true disciple must aim for one goal, have only one ideal, one desire, one kind of food. Only in this way will he truly live in the light.

26. *Correct your mistakes at once*

Never let your inner feelings of malaise reach such proportions that you can no longer remedy them. Suppose you absent-mindedly step in some wet concrete and are so lost in thought that you neglect to step out of it again : what will the result be ? The concrete will harden ; in fact, it will become so hard that someone will have to go and get some tools to break it before you can get your feet free, and you may well be hurt in the process. Well, this is what happens in the inner life : if you fail to remedy your mistakes or faults very quickly, it will be too late. The remedy will be very costly and may well cause further damage.

27. *Close your doors to lower entities*

Our weaknesses are like so many doors, and entities that have the intention to harm us try to slip into us through them. When we give in to certain weaknesses, we give these entities the right to sneak in and torment us. If we stand up to them and refuse to give in, they have no power over us. This is why I say that negative entities have only the power that you, yourself, give them. If you want to have nothing to do with them, don't open your doors to them ! They never force you ; they only make suggestions and it is you who accept their suggestions. Most people imagine that their misfortunes happen all at once, out of the blue, but that is false : they have prepared them themselves ; they have opened their doors and invited them in. How ? By giving in to greed or other weaknesses, by transgressing certain laws. It is when people do these things that they open their doors and demons slip in. Be careful, therefore, keep your doors firmly closed against them.

28. Our ideas determine our actions

You say that you never relax your efforts to transform yourself but that you have nothing to show for it ; that all your good resolutions do no good. Don't be discouraged ; a profound transformation cannot be achieved all at once : it takes time. Sooner or later, if you keep your good resolutions constantly in mind, you will end by behaving in accordance with your desires.

Watch a snake going into its hole : the head goes in first and, however long its body may be, the tail is bound to follow in the end. But, as a snake moves in a sinuous curve, the tail often seems to be going in the opposite direction to the head ; in the long run, though, it always goes exactly where the head has gone : head and tail are not separated from each other and the tail always follows the head. Symbolically, the head represents the faculty of thought and reason, the ability to decide on an orientation, and the rest of the body, which represents the practical application, the concrete realization, necessarily follows the lead of the head. This is why it is such an advantage to cultivate the right kind of thoughts : even if your actions don't fully correspond to your thoughts yet, if you persevere in a good mental attitude, you will end by overcoming all your inner resistance and acting in obedience to the spirit.

You have still not fully grasped how important it is to have a good philosophy. Many people imagine that they can let any kind of thoughts enter their minds without it affecting their behaviour. That is because they don't realize that the tail always follows the head. Pay attention to this question, therefore : every day you must scrutinize the thoughts that you allow into your head because, if they are anarchic and immoral, sooner or later your behaviour will be anarchic and immoral also. This law applies both to evil and to good.

29. Your efforts
are more important than the results

What counts in the eyes of Heaven is not so much your successes as your efforts, for only your efforts keep you on the right path ; your successes are liable to make you less vigilant. Even if your efforts are not crowned with success ; even if you seem to get no results, it doesn't matter : at least you have been working.

Don't ask for success, therefore ; it doesn't depend on you but on Heaven, and it will come when Heaven decides that the time is ripe. The only thing that depends on you is to make an effort, for Heaven cannot make it for you. Just as no one else can eat in your place, Heaven cannot eat — that is to say, cannot make your efforts — for you ; it is up to you to make them. But where success is concerned, it is a different matter : Heaven decides when and how it will come, according to what is best for your evolution.

Actually, our efforts contain their own reward. After every effort, every exercise of the mind, life takes on a different colour and a different flavour. Work, therefore, without trying to set a deadline for the achievement of your spiritual aspirations. If you decide that you will obtain this or that result in your inner life or conquer this or that weakness by a specific date, you will only succeed in becoming tense and your spiritual development will be less harmonious. You must work towards perfecting yourself but without setting a time limit ; work in the thought that you have eternity ahead of you and that, sooner or later, you will achieve the perfection you long for. Let yourself dwell only on the beauty of the work you have undertaken and tell yourself, 'It is so beautiful that I don't care how many hundreds or thousands of years it takes to complete it !'

30. Accept your failures

If someone sees that he is not capable of manifesting the qualities that he has been working at, he must not give way to discouragement or revolt. He must be humble in the face of failure, otherwise it means that he is not reasoning correctly, and this is always because his lower nature has managed to slip in when conditions were right. When you fail, it is as though Heaven sent certain entities or circumstances to you, telling them, 'Go and nip at him ; go and tease him ...Let's just see what happens.' And what happens is a turmoil that proves that you were not ready for trials. Failure should neither sadden nor discourage you ; if it does, that simply shows that you are conceited enough to expect something that is still out of reach and, if you don't overcome your diappointment, you will end by destroying yourself. You are permitted to be sad, but only because of the lack of success or the misfortunes of others, not because you have failed to fulfil your own desires, ambitions or pretentious expectations.

Instead of rebelling or being discouraged if you are having great difficulty in acquiring a quality, conquering a failing or overcoming a bad habit, remind yourself that everything is more difficult because, in the past, you did not do your work properly. Tell yourself this and then get back to work, at once. Yes, even if you have only a year to live, only one year, you must keep working. Keep at it. You will see all the changes that come about if you do this, for, if we have tried sincerely to perfect ourselves, we take with us all the spiritual acquisitions that our efforts have earned.

31. The imagination
as a means in our work to improve ourselves

When we see how difficult it is to overcome our faults, we often feel unhappy and discouraged, whereas, instead of dwelling on our failings, which are the consequence of disorders we have indulged in in the past, we would do far better to turn our attention to the work that lies before us. Tell yourself, 'I'm going to rebuild and repair everything', and then, every day, with unshakeable faith and absolute conviction, work towards that goal. That is to say, take the elements that God has given you, your imagination and your thoughts and feelings, and re-create yourself, re-model yourself into what you want to be. Picture yourself surrounded by light, giving the support of your love and generosity to those who need it, and standing firm in the face of difficulties and temptations. Little by little, the images that you form of these qualities will come alive and influence you ; they will transform you and, at the same time, work to draw into you, from the universe, all the corresponding elements.

To be sure, it takes a great deal of time and work to produce results but you need never doubt that, one day, the results will show themselves. You will feel the presence of a living entity hovering over you to protect, instruct, purify and enlighten you and, when things get difficult, to give you the support you need. If you form this mental image of perfection for a long time, it will gradually descend and materialize on the physical plane.

32. Music as an aid to spiritual work

Learn to use music in your inner work ; it will help you to fulfil all your noblest desires. You wish for so many good things but you don't know what to do to achieve them. This is where music comes in : it can be a tremendous help in achieving concrete results. When you listen to music, instead of letting your thoughts drift aimlessly, focus on whatever it is you most desire. If it is health, for instance, see yourself as a being so full of health and vitality that, whatever you do, whether you walk or talk or eat, health radiates from you and makes everyone around you well. If light, intelligence, is what you need most, use music to help you imagine that you are learning and understanding, that light penetrates your being and that you amplify it and give it to others. And you can do the same thing for beauty, strength, will-power or perseverance. Work in this way in every area in which you feel a lack.

33. The beneficial influence of a spiritual collectivity

So many people sense that they are not on the right path ; their soul and conscience rebel against their way of life and they decide to change. To begin with, all goes well and, then, once again, they are led astray. Once again, they regret their weakness, they pray and decide to do better but, as before, their good intentions are short-lived. To be sure, it is already something to realize that one is on the wrong road but it is not enough : it is essential to persevere in one's good resolutions. This is why a spiritual collectivity, a spiritual brotherhood, is so necessary — indispensable, in fact — for our spiritual well-being : because it gives us the conditions we need to keep to the right road. When someone is tired and ready to abandon everything, he will be encouraged and stimulated by the sight of others who are persevering.

Apart from a few very exceptional cases, human beings need to be supported and stimulated, for there are always moments when their spiritual ardour flags. You will, perhaps, say that you have no desire to be influenced, that you wish to be free to do as you like and that, for this reason, you don't want to join a collectivity in which you would feel restricted. Well, this just shows how unintelligent you are. Someone who is intelligent knows very well that he needs to be protected, so he puts himself in a situation in which he will be prevented from doing anything foolish and free, on the other hand, to undertake luminous, beneficial activities.

34. Rely on nothing but your own work

As long as your activities do good and are disinterested, you can trust the divine laws : sooner or later, your efforts will receive their reward. Every word you utter, every gesture you make, every one of your thoughts and desires are recorded and classified and, one day, they will produce results. This is the law that you must count on : everything is liable to change except this law. Your friends can betray you, your family can be busy elsewhere and forget you, but this law will always be there to give

you exactly what you deserve depending on how you
have worked. Rely on nothing but your own work.

You will say, 'What about the Lord and all the
Angels and saints : can't we count on them to help
us ?' Yes, you can, but only if you have done your
own work. If you have not sown any seeds, however
much you call on the Lord to help you, you will
not get anything to grow. The Lord has instituted
certain laws and it is up to human beings to know
them ; He is certainly not going to upset the order
of the universe in order to please somebody who
is ignorant because he has chosen not to know them.
Sow a seed and all the laws of the universe will contribute to making it grow. And this means that you
must rely, first and foremost, on your own work
and, secondly, on the Lord, that is to say, on the
laws of the universe.

35. *Live in an atmosphere of poetry*

When you go into the streets or into offices and
shops, when you take a train or a bus, wherever you
go, almost all the faces you see are gloomy, sad,
tense, aloof or hostile. It is not a sight to gladden
your heart ! In fact, even if a person has no reason
to feel sad or out of sorts to start with, he cannot
help but be affected by such a negative atmosphere
and, as likely as not, he will go home with a feeling
of malaise which he will pass on to his whole fam-

ily. This is the deplorable kind of life that human beings continually create for each other. Why do they never make an effort to show others a bright, open, smiling face ? They don't know how to live a poetic life thanks to which they would be a constant delight to others. True poetry is not confined to literature ; true poetry is a quality of the inner life. Everyone appreciates the arts, painting, music, dance, sculpture, etc., but why don't they bring their lives into harmony with the colours, rhythms, forms and melodies they love ?

The thing we look for and love in people is their quality of poetry : we need to see, feel and breathe something ethereal and luminous, something that soothes, harmonizes and inspires us. But as so few understand this, almost everybody goes through life without a thought for the painful impression they make on others. There they are, looking thoroughly grouchy and ill-humoured, frowning and tight-lipped, with an expression of distrust in their eyes ; and even when they employ various stratagems to make themselves more appealing, the flatness and dreariness of their inner life cannot help but transpire.

Henceforth, therefore, you must no longer leave poetry to the poets who write it. It is your life that must be poetic. Yes, the true *art nouveau* is to learn to create and diffuse poetry all around oneself, to be cordial, expressive, luminous and vibrant.

36. Self-knowledge is indispensable to success

If you don't know yourself well, if you are not lucid about your strengths and weaknesses, your qualities and defects, you will never succeed in what you undertake and, especially, you will never be able to live harmoniously with other people ; your ignorance will inevitably lead to complications, conflict and quarrels. In fact, it would be true to say that most of the difficulties people meet with in their everyday lives stem from the fact that they don't know themselves. The one subject about which people delude themselves most is their own worth, their own character and abilities, and this ignorance can be very grave ; it can expose them to great dangers. Everything you undertake in your personal and social life will be in danger of coming to grief if it is not based on a lucid appreciation of your character and abilities.

37. Start off on the right foot

The quality of your work, the successes you achieve or the defeats you suffer all depend on your state of mind and the intentions that motivate you when you take the first step in a new undertaking. You will, perhaps, think it strange that a whole series of circumstances should depend on one little detail, but you only have to look carefully at yourself to see the truth of what I say. If you are in a state of agitation when you set out to meet someone, you will stir up chaotic forces around you ...and then what happens ? Suppose that you have to settle a rather delicate matter with the person you are going to see : while you are on your way, the forces you have stirred into action will do their work of destruction within you and, by the time you reach your destination, your state of mind will have gone from bad to worse. How can you expect to settle anything in these conditions ? Whereas, if you try to achieve an inner state of calmness and serenity and great love and set out in that frame of mind, the nearer you get to your destination the better will be your inner state and the greater your chances of concluding your business satisfactorily. This is what it means to 'start off on the right foot'.

38. Avoid expressing your dissatisfaction

Very few people realize how terribly destructive it is always to be dissatisfied with everything and everyone and to create a climate of disharmony wherever one goes. Dissatisfaction is acceptable only if it is aimed at oneself. Someone who never stops complaining and expressing his displeasure with God, life and the rest of the world, must be warned that this destructive attitude will lead him to make all kinds of mistakes. And, as a discontented man cannot prevent his feelings from showing, his face

will become sombre, his eyes lacklustre, his voice
harsh and his gestures brusque ...all of which will
make him very unattractive to others. For, although
people tend to see discontent as a sign of intelligence, they don't find it easy to get on with those
who are always discontented. In fact, they tend to
keep well away from them. How can anyone take
pleasure in the company of those who never open
their mouths without criticizing and poisoning
the atmosphere with their complaints and
recriminations ?

39. Never go empty-handed to others

In every country in the world it is the custom
to take a present when you go to visit someone. This
is a very ancient tradition based on a law according
to which one must always have the desire to give
something when one approaches others. If you are
always empty-handed, physically or symbolically,
when you go to see your friends, they will end by
losing all affection for you. They will say, 'What
kind of a man is he ? He is always empty when he
comes and, by the time he leaves, he has emptied
me, too'. They will begin to be wary of you and
keep you at arm's length and, in the long run, close
the doors of their heart and soul to you completely. Don't go and see your friends if you cannot even
take them a smile, a kind look, a few warm words,

for these are gifts that are alive. You must get into the habit of giving, of giving that which is most beneficial to others. If you know how to work with the positive forces of nature, others will love and appreciate you.

And since every gesture has magical significance, never greet someone with an empty container in your hand, especially in the morning, because, without meaning to do so, you will be wishing him emptiness, poverty and failure for the rest of the day. If you really have to carry an empty container, put something into it. It doesn't have to be anything valuable ; it can be water — which is the most precious thing there is in the eyes of the Creator — or anything else, and then you can greet your friends with the thought that you are bringing them gifts of health, fulfilment and happiness.

Never forget that you have a magnificent garden within you and that you can distribute your flowers and fruits to everyone you meet. If you have this desire always to give something of your own soul and spirit, life will never cease to flow within you.

40. The hand
is a means of communication and exchange

The importance of our hands is very evident in everyday life, because we use them to communicate with other people. When people meet or separate,

what do they do ? They raise their arm in greeting
or shake hands. This is why you should be extremely
careful about what you give with your hands. If you
greet someone it is in order to give him something
good. A person who is incapable of giving shows
how poor and wretched he is.

Of course, for many people, a handshake is an
empty, mechanical gesture : in this case, it would
be better not to make any gesture at all. But for
those who are fully conscious, it can be an extremely
significant, effective gesture by which they can encourage, console and vivify others and give them
a great deal of love. A greeting should be a true
communion ; it should be a cordial, harmonious
gesture. When you shake a person's hand you
should feel the current passing between you ; to do
this, as you are giving him your hand, wish him
health, peace and light and breathe deeply (discreet-
ly, of course !), for a deep breath will make your
exchange harmonious.

41. Let your eyes radiate divine life

Most human beings have learned to control their
words and gestures to a certain extent : they don't
start punching every individual who irritates them
or kissing everyone who attracts them ; they don't
tell everyone with brutal frankness exactly what they
think of them. But they have still not learned to con-

trol their eyes, and their glances continue to express lust, sensuality, contempt or hostility. No one has ever been condemned for a look, because its effects are not as visible on the physical plane as those of a gesture or a word, and yet, what havoc a look can cause on the subtle plane !

To look is to project forces and energies, and these forces and energies may be either beneficial or destructive, dark or luminous. This is why you must learn to control and educate your glance so that its effects will always be beneficial. The spiritual life also begins with the education of your eyes. Just as the sun looks at us and sends us vivifying waves of light, every day, always try to look at people with light and disinterested love. Wherever you go, try to transmit a few rays of divine life to all those you meet by looking at them with unclouded sincerity and warmth.

42. Don't talk about your trials and tribulations

In the belief that your trials and tribulations are bound to interest people and touch their hearts, you continually let everybody know about them. But others have only one idea in mind when they see you coming : how to get rid of you as quickly as possible ! Yes, unfortunately — or fortunately — human nature is like that : if you want to scare everybody off, keep talking about your illnesses and

all your worries and sorrows, and you will soon see
how many people listen ! What a stupid attitude this
is ! You would do much better to keep quiet about
all those details. Generally speaking, other people
are not capable of helping you to find solutions to
your problems, so why talk about them ? They can't
do anything about them and the result is that, not
only do you waste your time by talking about your
private life to no purpose, but you lower yourself
in other people's eyes and lose their esteem. They
realize that you are neither intelligent nor strong and
they try to avoid you.

If you want to keep your friends, hide your
troubles from them ; don't talk about them, don't
complain. Instead, turn to the Heavenly Powers
above, to all those entities of light that are there,
ready to give you the help you need. When you do
this, you become stronger and more powerful and
luminous, and the strength and light emanating
from you will attract others ; they will see that you
are not like everybody else, that you bear your difficulties and trials without complaining. They will
admire you for this and turn to you in the desire
to imitate you and even draw strength from you ;
in this way they will be your friends for all eternity.

However great your difficulties may be,
therefore, don't burden others with them. Thanks
to your efforts to be disinterested, generous and
courageous, not only will you solve your problems

more easily, but Heavenly entities will see the gigantic work you are doing on yourself and come and help you.

43. Avoid criticism — Speak constructively

Many people have never learned to control their thoughts and feelings and are always ready to say all kinds of things about others. You must realize that this is a very serious matter for, if you slander someone and take away his good name or cast a slur on his honour, the consequences may be very detrimental to him and to his evolution, and Heaven will hold you responsible. To be sure, you will probably say, 'I didn't really mean it ...' Perhaps not, but you must realize that malicious spirits get hold of our negative words and, sooner or later, cause them to materialize. Our words are the material medium they need in order to carry out their evil designs. It is not they who are to blame, it is up to us not to supply them with the means to do evil.

You must be on your guard, therefore : as soon as you realize that you have gone too far in your criticism or accusations, you must immediately try to find other words, other thoughts and forces capable of repairing the damage you have done. This is the only way to be sure that the law will acquit you. Make it a rule never to end a conversation on a negative note : if you have been obliged to say something justifiably critical about someone, always try to end by saying something positive about him. There is always some good in every human being ; think of at least one of his good qualities, mention it, and then say no more.

A good way of evaluating yourself and your degree of evolution is to analyse your words : do you speak thoughtlessly or venomously about others ? Is what you say disjointed or exaggerated ? Do you speak out of self-interest ? Once you have analysed yourself, be on your guard and, before saying something, ask yourself why you want to say it : is it in order to do good, to enlighten, heal or liberate someone, or is it because you want to lead them astray, settle an old score or humiliate them and, in this way, gratify the tendencies of your lower nature ? In this case you would do better to keep quiet. In any case, it is generally better to talk less. It is often by their words that people hold themselves back and hinder their evolution.

Pay attention to this question in the future, therefore. When you are with other people, always try to choose useful, constructive subjects of conversation so that each person may go home thinking, 'Bless them for all their good words which have renewed my courage and allowed me to see things in a better light, which have strengthened my desire to stick to the path of light !'

Man's tongue was not given to him to be used as a means to belittle or annihilate others. Its mission is to help those who have fallen to pick themselves up, to enlighten those who are in darkness, to guide those who have lost their way. The tongue was given to man for the sole purpose of blessing, giving thanks and communicating with others in wisdom, justice and love. Sooner or later, in this incarnation or the next, those who don't realize how great a treasure they possess will lose it.

44. Be moderate in your choice of words

Always speak with prudence and moderation ; don't use big words ; don't commit yourself rashly to a course of action, for there is a danger that you will find it extremely difficult to keep your word.

A man swears that he will never have anything to do with a certain person or that he will never behave like another, whose actions he condemns, and yet, before long, we see him doing exactly what he condemned so vehemently. Why is this ? Because there are entities in the invisible world who, seeing that this man is so sure of himself, decide to find out just how strong he really is by putting him to the test and tempting him ...and he very soon succumbs. This is why so many people do just the opposite of what they had solemnly declared or promised. In some countries, people are in the habit of touching wood when they say certain things, as though to ward off an evil spell. This may seem superstitious but it is significant : it shows that people sometimes realize, subconsciously, that it is risky to assert something with too much confidence.

45. *Every promise is a bond*

When you make a promise you must be sure to keep it. A lot of people make beautiful speeches and promise all kinds of marvellous things, because it doesn't cost them anything to do so. Of course, it is much easier to say something than to do it, and some people think that, once they have promised something, they can forget about it : why should they keep their word ? Well, let me tell you that Initiatic Science teaches that a promise is like a signature, a commitment, a contract. Your words are recorded on the etheric plane and a spoken promise binds you just as surely as a written one. Nothing and nobody in the world can release you from it except those to whom you made it. If they are noble and understanding, they may release you but, if they refuse, you will have to go through with it. You will say, 'I'll ask God to release me from my promise', but even the Lord won't do so, because He cannot go against the laws that He Himself has decreed.

It is up to you, before making a promise, to be sure that you will be able to keep it. You must never say, 'Pooh ! I might as well promise ; it can't hold me to anything'. On the contrary : on the physical plane, if you have not committed yourself in writing, there may be no proof that would allow a court of law to condemn you but, on the subtle plane, your words still bear witness against you. The proof is not a piece of paper, it is a talking picture. Yes, you and your words have been recorded.

46. The magic of words

Learn to speak gently and lovingly, not only to human beings but also to animals, flowers, birds, trees and the whole of nature, for this is a divine habit. He who knows how to utter words that inspire and vivify possesses a magic wand in his mouth, and his words will never be spoken in vain, for at least one of the four elements is always there, ready and waiting to clothe his words in matter. The materialization may actually occur a long way from he who produced the seed, but you can be sure that it will always occur. Just as seeds are blown away by the wind to fall and take root in distant places, our good words fly from us and produce their magnificent fruits far from our sight. If you have learned to control your thoughts and feelings, if you have managed to attain an inner state of harmony, purity and light, your words will produce waves that will have a beneficial effect on the whole of nature.

47. A vital contact with nature

Our hands are a means of communication with other human beings and they can also be a means of communication with nature. This is why, when you open your door or window, in the morning, you should salute the sky, the sun, the trees, lakes and stars ...the whole of nature. You ask, 'What is the point of doing that ?' The point is that this gesture puts you in direct contact with the source of life, for nature responds when we greet her. When you first step out of doors, in the morning, or when you pass a lake, a mountain or a forest, greet them and talk to them. Talk to nature and to the Angels of the four elements, the Angels of air, earth, water and fire, and even to the gnomes, water-sprites, sylphs and salamanders. And greet the trees, the rocks and the wind, also.

Try it. As soon as you do so you will feel yourself becoming inwardly more symmetrical and harmonious : many dark, obscure elements will leave you, simply because you have made up your mind to greet living nature and her creatures. The day you are capable of maintaining a living bond with the whole of nature, you will feel true life flowing into you.

48. *Choose what will help your evolution, not what comes easily*

Consciously or unconsciously, human beings always tend to cut short certain states of mind and prolong others. If you are unhappy or in pain, you want it to end quickly, and if you are happy, you would like it to go on for ever. This is absolutely normal but, unfortunately, this tendency does not always manifest itself at the right moment or in the right direction. When it is a question of working, of making an effort, of reflecting or of communicating with Heaven, you are always in a hurry to finish. But, when you are eating and drinking, amusing yourself or doing something that gives you pleasure, you find that it is all over much too soon. Well, this is not how a truly spiritual person behaves. When a spiritual man recognizes that a sensation which gives him pleasure cannot make him inwardly richer, he will give less time to it or, even, put an end to it altogether. When it is a question of working or making a special effort, on the contrary, he will try to go on with it for longer. For he understands that immense treasures are buried deep within every effort, whereas joys and pleasures can so easily dull his faculties, keep him in a state of weakness and turn him from the truth.

Whenever you have to decide whether or not to engage in some activity, therefore, get into the habit

of asking yourself, 'What bearing will this have on
my spiritual progress ?' If you see that it will not
be much help in that respect, that it is more likely
to be a waste of time and energy, put it aside. Life
puts all kinds of temptations in your way and if you
have not acquired sufficient self-control to resist
them you will end by regretting that you have
weakened and defiled yourself. You could avoid a
great many mistakes if, before embarking on a new
adventure, you said to yourself, 'Granted that, if
I do thus and so, I shall be satisfying my desires,
but what effect will my behaviour have on myself
and those around me ?' Someone who never
asks himself this will always be surprised by what
happens to him. But he should not be surprised :
he could easily have known in advance what would
happen, for the consequences of our actions are
always foreseeable.

49. Obstacles help us to make progress

Stop complaining about the difficulties and
obstacles that you meet in life, because it is they
that enable you to advance. Why can ships sail on
water and planes fly in the air ? Because water and
air offer resistance. Nothing can advance if there
is no matter to offer a certain resistance. The
obstacles and difficulties in life play the same role
as water and air ; they are part of the natural order

of things and it is up to us to learn how to use them in order to make progress.

If you have done any rock climbing you know that it is the asperities and rough edges that afford a foothold and make it possible to climb higher, so, why do you want your life to be smooth and without asperities ? If it were, you would never reach the peak and, above all, think how easily you would slide all the way down ! Fortunately for you, life is full of bumps and rough places and it is thanks to them that you are still alive. Yes, this is why you should not ask for a smooth, comfortable life without suffering or sorrows, without enemies, for then you would have nothing to hang on to and help you to climb up, and you would keep sliding down. Those who ask for a life of ease and opulence don't realize that they are asking for their own downfall.

50. Don't run away from effort and responsibility

Those who think that they can avoid their responsibilities and obligations and lead an agreeable, carefree life don't know the severe laws that rule man's destiny. A man finds his family disagreeable, his job too taxing and the people around him boring, and makes up his mind to abandon them. Another shuns all social responsibility. A woman tires of her husband and looks for someone more entertaining and more alluring. Well, this kind of attitude is highly undesirable. Of course, there is no absolute law against leaving your job, your friends or, even, your family, if you have fulfilled all your obligations to them. If you haven't, the law will oblige you to meet all these people that you could not bear and to live with them again. If you want to be sure of not having to meet someone again, pay all your debts to him and you will be rid of him for ever. People don't know this law. They do everything they can to get away from someone they dislike, to cut their ties with parents, wife or children, without realizing how often the law of karma obliges human beings to live with the same people again, in another incarnation.

If fate has placed us in certain circumstances, it is because there is a reason. We must learn to be undefeated by the difficulties of the world around us. How can we do this ? In the same way as athletes, who train every day, or as explorers, mountaineers or seamen, who learn to put up with heat and cold, fatigue and lack of sleep or food, to endure fearful weather conditions and survive great dangers. This is what you have to do, too : train yourself to endure, to survive, not so much physically, of course, as psychically and morally. Of course, if, at some point, you find yourself incapable of putting up with your situation any longer, get away from it for a while ; but keep coming back to face up to it again until you are really strong.

If you are capable of choosing the difficult path, the Lord will send Angels to help you but, if you choose the path of facility, you will be obliged, sooner or later, to start all over again and assume all the responsibilities that you ran away from.

51. *Apologies are not enough ; we have to make good our mistakes*

When you have done someone a wrong, it is not enough to apologize : you must also make reparation. This is the only way to be free of your debt. To say, 'I'm terribly sorry ; do, please, forgive me !' is not enough, and divine Law will pursue you until you have repaired the damage you have done. You will say, 'But what if the person I have injured forgives me ?' It is not quite so simple : the law is one thing and the person another. The person may forgive you but it is not the role of the law to forgive you ; it will pursue you until you make full reparation. Of course, when a person forgives an injury, it shows that he is capable of nobility and generosity and the gesture frees him from the torments and sorrows that bound him to the lowest astral regions. If Jesus told us to forgive our enemies, it was because that is the only way for man to free himself from the corrosive effects of his own resentment and bitterness. But forgiveness does not put an end to the matter ; it releases the victim of wrong-doing

but it does not release the perpetrator. He will only be released when has atoned for the wrong he
has done.

52. Difficulties help to develop intelligence

For someone who knows how to make use of
them, the difficulties of life provide the most
favourable conditions for growth. Unfortunately,
instead of studying these difficulties and trying to
find ways of overcoming them, most people do
nothing but grumble and groan about them. This
shows that they have never understood why our
brains are in the highest part of our bodies. If they
understood this, instead of suffering and weeping
and spending all their time on the lower level, in
the heart and the emotions, they would try to rise
to the level of reason, intelligence and light.

When you feel like crying, tell yourself, 'Very
well, I'll let you cry ; in fact, here's a handkerchief
all ready for you, but wait a minute or two ; I have
to think.' Then you apply your mind to finding a
solution, and you may be sure that you will find
it. In fact, you will find it much more quickly than
if you let yourself be carried away by your emotions.
Otherwise, you can give way to tears for hours, until
you are thoroughly exhausted. After that, you will
be calmer, no doubt, but you will be no nearer a
solution ; on the contrary, your energies will be

diminished and your difficulties will still be as large as life. And the whole thing will begin, all over again, the next day. Instead of allowing yourself to be dominated by your feelings, therefore, put them to one side and try to reach another region of yourself, the spiritual region which is pure reason, pure wisdom and pure light.

Twenty or thirty times a day you have the opportunity to practise this and, if you use each occasion to its fullest advantage, many apparently unpleasant circumstances can be made to contribute to your good. Life has an abundant supply of all that is needed for the instruction of human beings. The wise reflect about everything, learn from everything and use everything for good. Others, those who don't possess the light, take advantage of nothing ; in fact, when good things do happen to them, not only do they fail to recognize or exploit them, they even manage to turn them against themselves. If you are fully conscious and vigilant, therefore, you will know how to make use of all your trials and difficulties so that they contribute to your evolution.

53. *There is a key for every problem*

Suppose that, yesterday, you managed to find a solution to one problem and then, today, another one arises : you will almost certainly not be able to use the solution you used yesterday, for each different problem demands a different solution. Every door in your house has a lock and key. You cannot unlock all the doors with the same key ; you have to find the right one for each door. This is true in our psychic life also : there are different keys that must be used to open different doors. If you always try to use the same key, you will find yourself perpetually in front of doors that refuse to open. The three essential keys are love, wisdom and truth : love opens the heart, wisdom opens the intellect and truth opens the will. When you are looking for the solution to a problem, you have to try the different keys one after the other. If the first one won't unlock the door, try the second, and if that one doesn't work, try the third.

Every day, we need to eat and drink, sleep, have a roof over our heads, clothe ourselves, work, move about, read, listen to music, meet people, reflect, love, admire …All these needs have been given to us by Cosmic Intelligence and they all represent different problems to which we have to find solutions and, in this way, grow and develop in every area and on every plane. As soon as a new need manifests itself, a new problem arises, followed by another and then another and, each time, we have to try to find a solution that fits the problem.

New needs are constantly making themselves felt in the world, giving rise to new problems and, therefore, to new activities. It is life itself that causes this, because, as life flows and circulates, it displaces things, and man is obliged to swim with the current and to go past one place and then another ...or else he has to change the direction of the current, as has already been done for certain rivers. Life does not allow us to stagnate ; it obliges us to flow with it, passing all kinds of different places as we go and, in this way, we learn to see, understand, feel and act in all the different ways possible. This is why we must always do our best to find solutions to the new problems that life confronts us with and, I repeat, each problem can be put into one of three general categories according to whether they concern the will, the heart or the intellect ; or, if you prefer, the body, the soul or the spirit.

54. Don't dwell on the inconveniences of life

To fly into a rage because someone has been rude to you, something you buy costs more than you had expected, the soup is too salty or someone has borrowed something from you and then lost it, and to react to these minor inconveniences as though they were major catastrophes is a very stupid attitude. You must learn to weigh all the irksome little details of life against the tremendous gifts that Providence has distributed so abundantly. Instead of this, people do just the opposite : they continually compare their own meagre possessions with the abundance of their neighbour's. 'He can afford a car, and I still have only a bicycle !' or 'Her diamonds are real, and I only have false pearls !' If you are so determined to make comparisons, why not compare all the advantages you have with the poverty, illness or unhappiness of others ?

You tell me that you have every reason to be discontented, because everything you undertake fails, you have no future, etc., etc. The truth is that the days are not all the same : if the sky is full of clouds today, tomorrow you will see the sunrise, and everything will smile on you again. 'It's too late', some of you will say, 'I'm already old. What hope is there for me ?' But don't you know that you will come back to earth again as a baby, to begin a new life, enriched by all your past experiences, and that all your hopes will live again ?

There is an answer to every objection raised by sadness and discouragement, but you will not find it unless you accept to look at things differently, and this requires that you reason correctly. Every time a new situation or event crops up, take the time to consider both the negative (since you insist !) and the positive aspects. It is, obviously, no good deluding yourself and saying that everything is perfect but, at the same time, you must refuse to look only on the dark side of life. You are think- ing, 'Oh, we know all that, already !' Do you ? In that case, why don't you do it ? It is so simple. Observe your behaviour and you will see that you too often forget to put your good notions into practice.

55. *Suffering is a warning*

Nature has placed entities within us to watch over us and, when we start to destroy something in our physical bodies or in our hearts or minds, these entities sting and bite us in order to get us back onto the right path. This is what suffering is : a warning that we have strayed from the good conditions in which things were clear and easy.

Suffering, therefore, is an entity sent by the Invisible World to save us and we must not fight against a saviour. The more one fights suffering the worse it gets. It says, 'Ha, you don't want to understand, is that it ? Well, I'll show you !' and its attacks grow more violent. But, when you understand and decide to mend your ways, suffering is ordered to retreat, because it has done its work ; its mission is accomplished. Instead of rebelling and struggling against suffering, therefore, you should put your ideas in order and say to the Lord, 'Lord, I see, now, that it is the senseless way I have been living that has brought me to this ; now that I understand I have decided to change my ways. Please give me some credit, give me conditions that will help me to mend all that and dedicate myself to Your service.' This is the only thing to do. It is sheer stupidity to rebel against suffering ; it is not sent to us by chance, nor as a form of revenge or punishment ; it is simply a servant of God that is sent tc warn us.

Since it is impossible to avoid suffering, it is better to put up with it and advance rather than continuing to suffer and remaining the same. So many people suffer without understanding why. This is what is so awful : to be afflicted by all kinds of trials and misfortunes without ever understanding the reason, for things can go on like that for ever. Henceforth, try, at least, to understand *why* you suffer ; it is the only way to be free and make progress.

56. *Be grateful for your trials*

So many people react in a spirit of revolt when they have to endure trials. 'Why should this happen to me ?' they ask, indignantly. Well, that is just the point : it is happening to you and you must accept it and try to get from it all the elements which will be most useful to you for your spiritual growth. It is important to understand that the present stage of development of the earth and of human evolution makes it impossible for man not to suffer. The earth is both a reform school and a training centre. Suffering is inevitable, therefore, and when you accept it, it sets in motion hidden forces that accomplish great things within you.

When you are going through a very difficult period, remind yourselves that, since you are sons and daughters of God, you have the means you need within you to overcome this trial. You should love the trials that come to you. This does not mean that you have to be so stupid as to go out and look for them (they will come to you soon enough without your looking for them) ; it means that you have to come through them successfully and, in order to do that, you have to learn to be grateful for them, because they always have a reason, a meaning.

Believe me, when you rebel against divine justice, you increase your burdens. If you want to make them lighter you have to thank Heaven for them. 'What ?' you exclaim, 'You expect me to thank Heaven when I'm unhappy and ill and have no money ?' Yes, this is the great secret : even when we are unhappy we have to find a reason to be grateful. Are you poor and needy ? Give thanks and be grateful ! Be grateful that others are rich and have everything they need, and you will see the results ...It will not be long before certain doors will be opened and blessings will begin to flood into you.

To learn to be grateful for your trials is the best way to transform yourself. If you rebel against them, it is a sign of pride and you will be incapable of transforming those trials into gold and precious stones. Say, 'Thank you Lord, thank you ! There is certainly a reason why this should happen to me ; there is something I have to learn from this. I know that I must have done all kinds of stupid things …that I'm far from perfect'. Thanks to the humility that enables you to say this, you will immediately begin to feel better about things. Try it and you will see for yourselves.

It is important to understand that you have to use your difficulties and be glad of them, even if there is no apparent reason to rejoice. This philosophy will give you the power to overcome and rise above every difficulty, to float above life, to be in control of every situation. And, when Providence sees your power and strength of soul, it will remove certain obstacles from your path and spare you certain sufferings until, eventually, you are delivered from every obstacle or difficulty.

57. Difficulties
force us to rely on our own resources

The Invisible World sends us many trials and tribulations in life so that we shall be forced to count on the spiritual forces within us. When we are rich, contented and comfortable, we tend to remain on the surface of things but, when we are lonely and unhappy, we are obliged to find new resources within ourselves. The function of Initiation is to teach man to enter into himself in order to find true wealth, true strength and the true support he needs. In ancient times, Initiation was given in the temples but, today, it is given in our everyday lives, just when we are least expecting it. Perhaps you are wondering, 'Why doesn't the Invisible World give us advance warning of the trials we are going to have to endure ?' Precisely because, when we are taken by surprise, we are obliged to enter more deeply into ourselves and make a greater effort.

You will all have trials to endure and you must be glad of it, for they all help to make you richer. Those who have never suffered are very poor, they have no pigments with which to paint their pictures — symbolically speaking. But those who have suffered can use all the sensations they have experienced to paint pictures. Great geniuses and all those who have achieved something in their lives, have suffered greatly. They possessed some black ink, and it is from that black ink that they produced the most beautiful colours.

58. Remember that your misfortunes are temporary

Whenever something really difficult comes up, think to yourself, 'This won't last. It's only temporary. It will soon be over.' Does this surprise

you ? Are you thinking that it can't possibly do any
good ? It can, I assure you ; I have used this method
myself and it is highly effective. The mere thought
that one's misfortunes are temporary helps us to put
up with them. Besides, it is perfectly true : they
won't last for ever. Twenty, thirty or, even, forty
years, perhaps, but that is not eternity ! You only
have to be patient. In any case, more often than
not, you have spent years getting yourself into the
inextricable situation you are complaining about.
You certainly showed a great deal of patience and
perseverance then, and you are going to have to be
just as patient in order to sort things out and repair
the situation, now. Good and evil both take time
to manifest themselves. Whatever trials you have
to endure, therefore, always remind yourself, 'It's
no more than a bad patch I'm going through ; it
will soon be over because, this time, I have the
means I need to rebuild my future and live it divine-
ly', and then get back to work.

59. Look upwards

When you experience difficulties, you are in the
habit of concentrating on them ; you begin to think
about them all the time, ruminating about all that
goes wrong, all that gives you cause for worry, an-
xiety and distress. This habit of looking down at
your problems is not a good way of dealing with

them : you must try to look upwards, towards the regions of light, wisdom and beauty, towards all that can give your soul the stimulus it needs to discover the means to overcome your difficulties. Cares and sorrow will always exist, you cannot hope to be spared, but you can deal with them if you equip yourself properly, just as we equip ourselves to deal with bad weather or mosquitoes. You protect yourself from the rain by using an umbrella, from the cold by wearing warm clothes or installing a heating system, from mosquitoes with mosquito netting or insecticide. And you can protect yourself from difficulties by looking up to a higher world and drawing down light and strength. This is the only way to overcome your difficulties.

60. The method of a smile

When you are out of sorts, perhaps because you have let yourself get slack, someone has offended you or you have had some bad news, there is a marvellous method available to you, and that is to use the power of a smile. Even if you are alone, try to show that you are above your difficulties by smiling. Remember that you are invulnerable, immortal and eternal, and smile at yourself in the mirror in passing. At the first attempt your smile may be a little crooked, but that doesn't matter, it will be the beginning of an improvement for, behind the method of the smile, is the method of love. As soon as you opt for this method, you will feel in a better frame of mind, and once you are in a better frame of mind, it will be easier to find solutions to your problems.

61. *The method of love*

When you are upset, anxious and unhappy, you must try to react. Instead of letting your worries devour you or bothering others with them, sit down quietly and begin by taking a few deep breaths. Then, say just one word with love, make a gesture with love, send out a loving thought. You will find that the things that were fermenting and rotting within you have been driven out and are already far away. By calling on love, you have released a spring within you and, now, all you have to do is let it flow and do its work ; it will purify everything. You see : it's easy ; you only have to open your heart and give love its head. Try this method and you will wonder why you have never used it before. People are always talking about love ; they joke about it and toy with it but they never use it as a means of salvation.

To live with love is to live in a very elevated state of consciousness which is reflected in everything you do ; it is a state which ensures that you are always in perfect balance and harmony, a state which is a source of joy, strength and health.

62. *The lesson of the pearl oyster*

How does the pearl oyster set about making a pearl ? It all starts with a grain of sand that gets into its shell and begins to irritate it. 'Oh, dear', says the oyster, 'This is terrible ; what a problem ! What can I do to get rid of it ?' So the oyster begins to reflect : it concentrates and meditates and asks for guidance until, one day, it realizes that it will never be able to get rid of the grain of sand but that it can wrap it up in such a way that it will be smooth, and shiny and velvety. And, then, when it has succeeded in doing this, it is very happy to have overcome its problem.

For thousands of years the pearl oyster has been there, as a lesson to human beings, but they have never understood it. And what does it teach us ? Simply that, if we wrap our difficulties and all the things that annoy us in a soft, luminous, opalescent matter, we shall be very rich indeed. This is what you have to understand. From now on, therefore, instead of complaining and doing nothing to prevent yourself from being worn down by your difficulties, set to work to secrete this special matter and wrap them up in it. Every time you have to put up with a painful situation or somebody you

really can't bear, be glad, and say, 'Lord God, what
luck, here's another grain of sand, another pearl
in view !' If you really understand this example of
the pearl oyster, you will have enough work to keep
you busy for the rest of your life.

63. *Learn to share your happiness*

There are days when you feel so rich and
happy that you float along in a state of bliss. When
this happens, do you think of sharing some of your
joy with those who are unhappy and in need ? You
must learn to give something from the abundance
you have received, saying, 'Dear brothers and sisters
throughout the world, I have been given something
so marvellous that I want to share it with you all.
Take some of this happiness ; take some of this
light !'

If you want to keep your happiness for yourself and are unwilling to share it, malicious spirits
from the invisible world will do all they can to take
it away from you ; they will provoke some un-
foreseen incident that will rob you of all joy and
happiness. If you don't want to lose your inner
riches, you have to share them with others. What
you give in this way will be credited to your account
in the banks of Heaven, and you will be able to
draw on it, later, when you need it. And all these
riches will always be within you ; no one can take

them from you, because you have put them safely away in the vaults of Heaven.

64. Don't let carelessness spoil your relationships

Let's say that you are talking to your employer, a business associate or a friend and, through carelessness and lack of self-control, you let slip a few unfortunate words and, before you know it, the damage is done : you are fired, the partnership breaks up or you lose a friend, with all the resulting complications and regrets. You say that you will try to repair the damage. Yes, you can try, but it is not always possible and, in any case, it will probably entail a great deal of time and effort. The sensible thing would be to understand from the beginning that, insofar as it depends on you, you must not let a lack of attention create complications of this kind. In the outside world, of course, there will always be some disorder and dissent, and there is not much you can do about it. It is not easy to establish peace in the world. But, in your own behaviour, at least, you can always try to preserve order and harmony.

65. Use love not force in settling your problems

When human beings have problems to settle with others, they always tend to resort to force. The result is that, far from being solved, their problems become even more complicated and corrosive, because this attitude triggers a reaction from their adversary's lower nature ; that is to say, a desire to hit back, to resist and, even, to exterminate the aggressor. As long as human beings continue to prefer brute force to the luminous power of the spirit, to the power of divine love, they will never find the answer to their problems. The only answer is in love, kindness and humility.

To be sure, this does not mean that everything will fall into place immediately, for if you treat others with kindness and humility, those who have been very badly brought up will consider you weak and stupid and will continue to trample you underfoot. But you must be patient. It will not be long before they realize that your attitude is not dictated by weakness but, on the contrary, by great moral and spiritual strength ; then they will begin to be humbler and more respectful and everything will straighten itself out. So try, from now on, to settle all your problems with your family, friends and enemies with love and kindness. When you do this, you trigger a law which obliges them to respond, sooner or later, in the same way.

When you meet anger with anger, hatred with hatred and violence with violence, you are applying a very old philosophy which has never given good results. The only remedy for viciousness is kindness, only love can drive out hatred, only by gentleness can you combat anger.

Get it into your heads, once and for all, that only good can combat evil ; this is a law, for good is strong and immortal and evil is weak. Evil is like a stone that you throw up into the air : with the passage of time, the upward thrust becomes rapidly weaker. Good, on the other hand, is like a stone thrown from the top of a tower : its downward movement accelerates with the passage of time. This is the secret of good : to start with, it is weak but it ends by being all-powerful. Evil, on the contrary, starts by being all-powerful but, with time, it weakens. It is very important to know this.

66. Learn to go beyond the law of justice

Don't think that, because someone has done you an injury, you have a right to revenge yourself on him. You will say, 'But I'm only asking for justice'. No, that notion of justice is the cause of all our troubles. In the name of justice, every Tom, Dick and Harry thinks that he has the right to punish others and teach them a lesson. Leave justice alone ! 'Well, what should we do instead ?' you will ask. You must have recourse to a principle beyond justice, a principle of love, kindness and generosity. It is two thousand years since Jesus brought this new Teaching to the world, and yet Christians continue to apply the law of Moses : 'An eye for an eye, a tooth for a tooth'. They have still not understood that man cannot be truly great or truly free if he continues to invoke the law of justice, if he continues to seek revenge. Revenge is an ancient, prehistoric method which solves nothing ; on the contrary, it only complicates things and increases our karmic debt.

Suppose you have been good to someone, you have helped and supported him, and then, one day, you discover that he did not deserve all that you have done for him. Well, you must just accept the situation : don't try to revenge yourself or punish him ...and don't go and tell everybody about it, either. When are you going to make up your minds to show a little generosity, a little nobility ? You must close your eyes to certain things, wipe them from your mind and forgive them ; this is the only way to grow and become stronger. In fact, you must know that all that you have lost will be given back to you a hundredfold. Otherwise, by trying to revenge yourself, you stir up so many negative forces that, sooner or later, there will be a backlash and it is you who will be annihilated.

In the meantime, if you really want to teach your enemy a lesson, forget about him and set to work to accomplish a gigantic transformation of yourself : pray, meditate, learn and practise until, at last, you possess true wisdom and genuine powers. Then, if you happen to meet your old enemy, he will be dumbfounded by the light and power that he senses in you ; he will realize that you have been working to become wiser, more generous and more in control of yourself while he has become more and more vile, and he will be ashamed of himself.

The only thing that really matters is for you to improve yourself, to concentrate only on what is constructive, pure and divine. Naturally, this demands a lot of love, patience and light, but I know of no more effective method. And, since there is a law which decrees that each person must pay for the evil he does, all those who have ever wronged you will be obliged, one day, to come and make reparation for their evil deeds. It is possible that, when this happens, you will sense intuitively that they have been your enemies and will want to put them off. But it will make no difference, they will continue to come to you and try to get you to accept their services. This is the law : those who have done you an injury, and to whom you have not responded in kind, will be obliged (whether they like it or not : their opinion doesn't enter into it) to come to you and make reparation for the wrong they have done you.

67. Be capable of a disinterested gesture

What a lot of time and energy you waste trying to get other people to respect your private property and what you consider to be your rights ! Why do you cling to your own interests with such tenacity ? For God's sake, do something disinterested for once ! You will find that this sets you free. To begin with, of course, you will not enjoy doing it, it will hurt and you will feel oppressed. But, if you manage to do it, you will discover new regions, new lights, and no one will be happier or prouder of themselves. Yes, because you will have done something very difficult ; you will have conquered your lower nature, which always urges you to fight for your material advantages.

If you count on wisdom and the love of Heaven, it will not abandon you ; as long as you do something that links you to Heaven, it will watch over you. Never lose faith in the power of the Invisible World : it sustains and supports all those who work according to its laws. If you follow the bad advice of your lower nature, you will never actually achieve your ambitions : sooner or later, the Invisible World will put obstacles in your way. But if you count on Heaven and respect its laws, you will never be abandoned. Even if the rest of the world abandons you, Heaven will always support and encourage and enlighten you.

68. Use your sympathies to bolster your courage and your antipathies to become stronger

A spontaneous sympathy or antipathy for certain people is a perfectly natural feeling that is experienced even by the sages. The great difference between a sage and an ordinary man, however, is that the sage overcomes his antipathies and does not trust his sympathies blindly. He knows that both come from an experience in a previous life with the people he encounters in this life, and that they cannot be relied on, therefore, to give him an impartial view of them. This is why he tries to be friendly to those for whom he feels a spontaneous incompatibility, and to recognize the errors and failings of those with whom he has an affinity.

And you, too, instead of unthinkingly allowing your sympathies and antipathies to guide you, you must learn to use them. When you have a spontaneous liking for someone, you can rejoice and draw courage from thinking of him, for those with whom you have an affinity influence you favourably and you can benefit from the good effect they have on you. 'And what about someone I disliked on sight ?' Well, there is something to be done, here, too : persuade yourself that you are going to overcome that dislike and, instead of avoiding him or thinking negative thoughts about him, practise putting up with him.

Simply by accepting to make this effort, it is you who gain, because you will be conquering your lower nature which is always so ready to precipitate quarrels, misunderstandings and complications. And, when your efforts are crowned with success, you enter a world of beauty and light, and it will not be long before you notice that everything has changed, for those whom you used to look at coldly and with hostility will see that you look at them differently and will begin to love you.

Believe me, there are always all kinds of opportunities for you to grow stronger. Why not make use of them ? You just accept your feelings of sympathy or antipathy and do nothing with them, and the point is that you could do something with them : they are natural impulses which you must use to advance your evolution.

69. The usefulness of enemies

Instead of feeling sorry for yourself when somebody is the cause of very unpleasant events that disrupt your life, try to understand why this happens. It is possible that that person was led to do whatever he did by the Invisible World in order to teach you a lesson, oblige you to understand certain truths or to mend your ways. In this case, why not take advantage of the occasion ? Instead of thinking about how to get your own back, rebelling against Heaven — which, in your opinion, should have exterminated your enemy long ago — or, even, as so often happens, wreaking vengeance on someone who is perfectly innocent, use the occasion to work on yourself.

This means that, even if someone behaves very badly with you, you must learn to behave well. And the first step in this process is to try to see what you can learn from unpleasant circumstances of this kind. The one thing that can harm you most is to foster negative feelings about others. For, as you must know, the currents of our psychic life go through our own being before reaching others. If we are moved by kind feelings, we shall be the first to benefit from that kindness and, if we are motivated by spite, we shall be the first to be poisoned. You say, 'I'm terribly angry with So-and-so ; I'm really going to let him have it !' Well, do as you please, but it is you who will be the first victim of your anger.

70. Transform evil

You must try to transform all the expressions of criticism and hatred that others send your way ; when they throw them at you they are like so many ordinary pebbles and you must learn to transform them into gems. This is true alchemy. If the earth can do this, why shouldn't we ? The essential thing

is to remember to do so. All forces and all powers
are contained in a human being ; he even possesses
the Philosophers' Stone, which has the power to
transmute all other metals into gold. Until you begin
to see things in this way, you will always feel ill-
treated and unhappy and you will be bowled over
by the slightest negative remark made about you.

71. The real enemy is within

So many people are in a permanent state of
revolt ! They are in revolt against a situation which
they find unbearable or against someone who seems
to them to be dishonest and unfair, etc. But is this
spirit of revolt particularly useful ? If you really
want to rebel, you can always find something that
it would be useful to rebel against in yourself. Yes,
don't you think that it is worth waxing indignant
and taking up arms against all your weaknesses and
baser tendencies ? If revolt exists in the universe,
it must mean that it has a role to play ; you cannot
simply do away with it. It would be much better
to understand its function and put it to work in the
service of your high ideal. When you do that, you
will know where, when, how and against what to
rebel. It is necessary to rebel, but only against all
those inferior entities, in the form of weaknesses,
that have taken possession of man and that deceive
and feed on him. Many of you are unhappy because

you are very aware of your faults and failings. Yes, but you are still not sufficiently in revolt against them to make up your minds to get rid of them, once and for all.

From now on, stop rebelling against your wife or husband, your employer or the government, etc., and start rebelling against yourself, for your real enemies are within. They are well camouflaged but they are constantly busy laying traps for you in the form of temptations, lusts and unrestrained desires. And, without realizing it, you caress and flatter and nourish them. Well, from now on, these are the enemies against whom you must rise up in revolt.

72. Awaken the good in others

Very few people have any inkling of how much damage they do with their mania for focusing on the negative aspects of people and things. Many friendships and human relationships are wrecked by this tendency to pick on other people's weaknesses, to dwell on all that is wrong or open to criticism and, even, to take pleasure in delving into people's private lives in the hope of discovering some guilty secrets.

A wise man endeavours to see both sides at the same time : the good and the bad. He is not blind, he has no illusions about people but he considers

that it is the good in them that matters, that this
is their essence. By focusing on the good, he attracts
and amplifies its forces both in himself and in
others. This is why people are always attracted to
someone like that : they can feel that the seeds of
their divine nature germinate and start to grow when
they are near him.

73. Live with love

It is love that provides the greatest possibilities
for success ; it is love that makes us more capable,
more lucid and more perceptive ; it is love that
prepares the right conditions for the most harmonious and constructive manifestations. But who
ever thinks about love ? Sexual love ...yes, of
course ; everybody is interested in that, but imper-
sonal, spiritual love is the last thing they think
about.

Some of you will object, 'You can't be living
in the same world ! Can't you see what human beings are like ? How can you possibly love them ?'
Let me tell you that none of you has experienced
what I have experienced : if there is someone who
knows how terrible life can be it is myself. But that
is just the point : even in these conditions, when we
have absolutely no desire to love anyone, because
— it is quite true — there is every reason to close

one's heart to human beings ...even then we must love. Otherwise, what use would Initiatic Science be ? What would be the point of this divine philosophy ? The fact that the world contains a few revolting specimens that we can't abide is no reason to deprive ourselves of love, this greatest of all blessings.

So, love ; love the whole world ; love all creatures. It is this love that will harmonize everything within you. Observe your reactions in all your different activities and you will see that your whole being is tense and on edge — your face and hands, particularly — and this tension is draining away your energies uselessly. All because you don't know how to work with love ! So, stop everything, relax completely. Above all, let your brain relax ; let it stop working for a few minutes and just allow yourself to feel love streaming through you.

The greatest secret, the most effective method is to love. When you leave your house in the morning, think of greeting all the creatures of the universe. Tell them, 'I love you, I love you ...', and then go off to work. For the rest of the day, you will feel happy and great-hearted, and your relations with others will be all the easier, because you have started the day by sending your love to every creature in the universe and, from every direction, that love comes back to you. There are so many different things you can do to make life worth living !

74. Become like a spring of water

Pure water wells up in a continuous stream from a natural spring and, even if people try to pollute it by throwing rubbish into it, it continually cleanses itself and washes all the dirt away. A spring is always pure and alive because never, for one moment, does it stop flowing. What better philosophy could you have than that of a spring ?

Model yourself on the spring, be like a spring. That is to say : love ; in spite of everything, never stop the flow of love. Your love will protect you from impurities and suffering ; if someone tries to slander or injure you in some way, you will not even notice it : the stream will simply wash it all away. Keep this picture of the spring that washes away all evils and impurities alive within you ; never stop loving and you will no longer suffer.

75. Heaven is generous with us
so that we may be generous with others

If some of the people you live with are very difficult to put up with, it is because you have to learn to love. One day, when you leave this world and come before the Heavenly Entities, they will ask you to account for yourself : 'Why didn't you love your fellow men more ?' 'Because they were ugly, vicious and stupid.' 'That is no excuse. Heaven gave you great riches ; eyes, a mouth, ears, intelligence, a heart, and so on ; and they were given to you so that, instead of speaking ill of others and despising and exploiting them and walking all over them, you should love them.' 'But they were such wretched creatures !' 'All the more reason to love them and be even more generous towards them.' Nothing you can say will excuse your lack of generosity.

76. Forget your enemies
by thinking of your friends

Has someone treated you unfairly or criticized or calumniated you ? Well, it's hard, I know, but why make yourself miserable by thinking about it for days on end ? Tell yourself, 'Even if some people don't love me, there are many who do ; the Lord loves me !' In this way, by thinking about your friends, about the divine world and about the Lord, who has created so many good and beautiful things that you are free to enjoy at every instant, you will forget all about the wrongs inflicted on you. If you make yourself practise this, you will become immune to all that is negative.

True sensitivity is to be totally open to Heaven and closed to all that is dark and negative. An acute sensitivity to what is negative is mawkishness, sentimentality, and it is an unhealthy manifestation of

the personality. What happiness can you hope for
if neither Heaven nor the Angels, neither flowers
nor birds nor friends exist for you, but only cruel,
unjust human beings ?

77. Learn to be strong in the face of criticism

Your enemies have criticized and slandered you,
and now you are completely demoralized. Why ?
Because you were not prepared. You have to
realize that it is going to be like that all your
life. What makes you think that you will be spared ?
The thing to do, now, is to pull yourself together
and tell yourself that this is not the last time
that you will be criticized, and that, if you do
nothing, today, to become stronger, next time it
happens you will be shattered all over again. Oh,
I know that this surprises you : you would like
to hear me say that it will never happen again ;
that, from now on, you will be spared and protected
from such things. But I cannot say that ; all I say
is that you must get ready for more trials of the
same kind. You must be ready, in advance, for all
kinds of unpleasant things to happen. If they don't
happen, thank Heaven for it ; and, if they do
happen, thank Heaven again, because at least you
will be prepared.

78. Learn to put yourself in other people's place

Very few human beings are in the habit of putting themselves in other people's place, and this is the cause of many cruelties and errors of judgement and of much injustice. People always cling to their own point of view : they measure and evaluate and judge everything according to their own tastes, tendencies and prejudices, without any consideration for others. But, now that modern means of communication make it so easy to be in touch with others, human beings must learn to break out from the confines of their own, limited awareness. If they fail to do this, all those things that could be used to bring them closer together will only serve to destroy them.

Before blaming others, therefore, try, if only for five minutes, to put yourself in their place. In doing this you will often realize that, if you were in their shoes, you would be ten times worse than they are. A few minutes of this exercise is sufficient to make you magnanimous, patient, indulgent and gentle with others. Try it for just a few minutes : put yourself in the place of all those you find so unpleasant and difficult to put up with, and you will see the results. You cannot help but understand and love them.

79. Some advice concerning children

Be careful about how you speak to them

Adults are never sufficiently careful about how they speak to children. Some people never stop calling them names : 'clumsy oaf', 'dunce' or 'idiot', and, as children are very suggestible, they are hypnotized by such treatment and really do become stupid and clumsy. You must realize that speech is an extremely powerful, active force and that what you say to children can inhibit and frighten them and do lasting damage. It is very often adults — parents or teachers — who ruin children. Why do they have to threaten them with a bogyman, a policeman, a wolf etc., in order to make them obey or do their work or keep quiet ? Children who are treated like that will feel threatened for the rest of their lives and become perfect subjects for psychoanalysis. There are a great many things that adults must correct in their attitude towards children.

How to develop a child's qualities

In order to be good educators, parents must think of all the qualities and virtues hidden deep in the soul and spirit of their child. It is not enough to spank your child in order to teach him not to do something wrong, you must focus on the spark of divine life in him and do everything possible to nurture it ; in this way, he will grow up to do wonders. When a child is asleep, the parents can stand by his bed and, without waking him, caress him gently and speak to him about all the marvellous qualities they want to see in him when he grows up. In this way, they plant precious elements in his subconscious and, when he discovers them years later, those elements will save him from many mistakes and dangers.

Create an atmosphere of harmony round your children

In order to educate a child, it is not enough to send it to school, however good that school may be. How can parents who constantly quarrel, lie and cheat in front of their children, expect them to turn out well ? It has already been demonstrated that a baby can fall ill and show signs of nervous disorders because of its parents' quarrels, even if it was not actually present. A baby, which still has a strong link with its parents, picks up the discordant atmosphere created by their quarrelling ; it is not conscious of this, of course, but the shock registers in its etheric body.

The behaviour of some parents is so extraordinary that one wonders if they really love their children. They, of course, will say that they do, but it is not true : if they loved them they would change their attitude ; at the very least, they would try to overcome certain weaknesses which have a very negative effect on their children. If they make no effort to do this it means that they don't really love them.

Be a perfect example for your children

Whatever the circumstances, parents must be irreproachable in front of their children ; they must show no weaknesses or faults. When children see their parents' or educators' weaknesses, it unsettles and confuses them, for they no longer know what to rely on. Children instinctively look for someone to lean on who incarnates justice, nobility and power ; they have an instinctive need for justice and truth and, when they see the adults who look after them doing something reprehensible, something within them is thrown off balance. Children sense that they are little and weak and need to feel the protective presence of an infallible authority. They may be ignorant, but this they know : that they are weak ; this is why they need protection and why they cling to their mothers, to feel their warmth. But it is not only on the physical plane that they look for someone to lean on, they have the same need on the psychic plane. This is why, when a child understands that his parents or teachers are not worthy of their role, he either feels lost or he rebels, and this is the root cause of so many tragedies in families and in society.

Certain conditions must be present if physical punishment is to be beneficial

Although it is better never to strike a child, an occasional little slap or even a real spanking will not do any harm. If you do have to administer a spanking, however, never do so in anger, for this can only leave an impression of hatred and cruelty instead of justice and, for the sake of the child's education, it is essential that he should feel that you are just and that it is precisely because you are just that you are punishing him.

For the same reason, when you punish a child, be very careful about the expression in your eyes. You must not look at him with anger or hostility or any other negative feeling, because he will soon forget a spanking but he will never forget your expression when looking at him.

Very often, adults slap a child because they are exasperated and have lost patience ; this is a very bad reaction. A child must never be punished simply because his parents are irritated — irritation is not an educational sentiment — but because they want to make him understand that, for his own good, he must learn to respect certain rules.

80. *The power of a disinterested word*

So many people, having demolished someone
with their criticism and censure, justify their
behaviour by saying, 'I only said it for his good ;
I wanted to help him, I was only being sincere'. It
would be truer to say that they had felt the need
to express their irritation or displeasure ; sincerity
is no more than a pretext. How is it that people suddenly become sincere when they are angry ?
However many good reasons you invoke in defence
of your action, the fact is that, as long as your
motives are not truly spiritual and disinterested,
your words will never have a good effect ; they will
be truly potent and beneficial only when you have
gained the mastery of your thoughts and feelings.
Until then, even if you would honestly like to help
others, not only will you fail to do so but you will
actually harm them or lead them astray.

81. *Gain a profound understanding of a truth*
      before talking about it

It is a rule of the spiritual life that, when you
receive a truth, you must put it into practice in your
life before trying to pass it on to others. Yes, this
is an important rule to remember : you have to experience a truth, to become familiar with it by
putting it into practice in your life until it has

become part of your very flesh and bones. When you are truly fused into one with it, nothing on earth will be able to make you lose it. Whereas, if you learn a truth and, the very next day, you start to talk about it indiscriminately, you are bound to lose it : if you bring it out and display it in the open market, it will no longer belong to you, and you will find yourself as weak and wretched as ever. You must begin, therefore, by keeping it to yourself and letting it strengthen you and help you to triumph over all your difficulties. If you do this it will never leave you again.

As long as you have not experienced a truth and applied it to your life, it cannot truly be a part of you ; this is why it is still possible to lose it and to have to suffer and struggle all over again to get it back. Keep it to yourself for a time, therefore, and live with it until it becomes yours ; if you do this, not only will it never leave you again but, when you do speak of it to others, your obvious sincerity will give it such force and power that you will convince them. The tone of your voice and the conviction emanating from you will be really persuasive, because you will have treasured that truth within yourself and, in doing so, you will have strengthened it.

82. Begin by reforming yourself

Human beings are always very quick to see other people's faults and failings, but not their own. They demand intelligence, kindness and honesty from others but it does not occur to them to wonder what they themselves are like. In fact, if there are so few people in this world who are perfect, it is because they all reason in the same way : they all expect others to make an effort to improve whilst they are convinced that they themselves need no improvement, they can stay as they are. The consequences of this attitude are extremely detrimental, especially to those who are responsible for others.

Take the case of parents, for instance : they look after their children and try to educate them, and that is only right ; it is their duty. But have they ever done anything to educate themselves before undertaking the education of their children ? No ; they have lived chaotic, disorderly lives and, now that they are thoroughly deformed and, even, dilapidated, they think that they are capable of bringing up children ! The fact that their children are going to be given the example of a deplorable way of life which will have a very negative effect on their psychological and physical health, is without importance. A great many people marry simply because they are bored with living alone and, then, when they have children, they find themselves in inextricable difficulties.

Before trying to educate others, look after your own education, otherwise it is like trying to remove a speck of dirt from a friend's face when your own hands are black with coal dust : you will simply make him dirtier than before. Those who start trying to enlighten and reform others without having reformed themselves first, can only lead them astray.

Leave everybody else alone, therefore, and concentrate on improving yourself. What is the point of moaning about the imperfections of mankind ? Pay no attention to that : give all your attention to getting rid of your own imperfections ; in that way, you will have less to worry about, you will stop wearing yourself out and your evolution will progress much more rapidly, because you will be concentrating on perfecting yourself.

Believe me, you must leave others to do as they please and work at yourself. It is you who must advance, you who must become an example for others. You will never reform others by preaching to them, however eloquently ; but if you are an example, they will follow you in spite of themselves. This is why, instead of expecting harmony to reign in your family, your neighbourhood and your place of work — and complaining when it doesn't — you must begin by achieving it within yourself. When others see how much you have changed they will be obliged to change, too, for it is contagious, it is magic : a human being who makes a sincere effort to transform himself releases forces that oblige those around him to do the same.

It is important to know the nature of human beings, to know what they really are and not pay too much attention to the aspects that inspire negative feelings in you, for there is a close correspondence between the things we pay attention to and our own state of mind. If you indulge in negative sentiments about others, don't be surprised to find yourself in a bad mood ; it is only to be expected. If you want never to be out of temper, worried or discouraged, you must learn to rely on nothing but your own, inner work.

83. The sun, our model of perfection

When you associate with a friend for whom you have great respect and admiration, without your being aware of it, you receive something of his qualities and defects. This is a law : we always end by resembling the people and things we admire. In the same way, if you get into the habit of looking at the sun, every day, and admiring its generosity, its power and the abundance of life that flows from it, you will gradually feel a transformation taking place in you, as though you were imbibing something of the sun's own light, warmth and life. The sun is the image of perfection and, if you take it as your model, if, like the sun, you think of nothing but spreading light, warmth and life, you will really and truly transform yourself. Of course, you will never achieve the same degree of light, warmth and life as the sun, but the desire to achieve it is enough to project you into celestial regions and you will really achieve great things.

If you want to have a beneficial influence on human beings, you must get in touch with the sun, every day, and ask it for new particles that you can then pass on to those around you. Only the sun has the power to give you what you need in order to love and help human beings. As long as you refuse to concentrate on this model of warmth and light, you will continue to manifest your lower nature. You only have to look at what goes on in the world : everybody is out to take advantage of and exploit and oppress others. And it is not a very glorious sight ! Whereas, in the sun, you have the image of a radiant, generous being and you cannot help but be influenced. Even if you consider that the sun is not capable of intelligence and reason in the ordinary sense of these terms, contact with its warmth and light necessarily inspires more brotherly feelings towards others, feelings of generosity, kindness and patience.

Take the sun as your model, therefore. During the course of the day, watch what you do and analyse yourself. Ask yourself, 'Am I radiating and spreading light ? Am I warming people's hearts and making them expand ? Am I communicating life to them ?' Yes, ask yourself these questions every moment of the day, for this is the key to perfection.

84. The secret of true psychology

The reason why people are so lacking in psychology is that they are too wrapped up in themselves. They are blinded by the veil of their lower nature which prevents them from discerning what goes on in the minds and hearts of others. Even when they love someone, this veil prevents them from seeing them clearly ; the result is that they are often astonished when they are suddenly aware of an unexpected transformation in their husband or wife, children or friends : they simply had not seen it coming. Only someone who has learned to forget his own interests can really know and understand others.

Here is a method you can use in order to rise above the limitations of your individual consciousness : in imagination, project yourself to a great height until you come close to the Being who embraces all beings, who contains and nourishes all beings within Himself. Ask yourself how He envisages the future of mankind and what plans He has for its evolution. When you try to get closer to this ineffably great and luminous Being, a secret work goes on in your subconscious, your consciousness and your superconsciousness, and the sensations you experience defy description. You must continue this exercise until you feel yourself melting into the ocean of light that is God. Once this practice has become a habit and you are able to enjoy moments of perfect fulfilment through your communion with the most exalted entities, you can begin to descend into the consciousness of human beings so as to understand them and feel for yourself their needs and their pain ; in this way you will be doing constructive work for the whole of humanity.

85. Look beyond appearances to the soul and spirit

Learn to have a sense of the sacredness of all men and women and, behind their clothes and the form of their faces or bodies, you will discover their spirits and souls which are sons and daughters of God. If you can learn to focus on their souls and spirits, all those you have ever neglected, abandoned or despised will become very precious in your eyes. Heaven itself, who sent them to earth in their present disguise, sees them as very precious beings and receptacles of the Godhead. This means that you must not pay attention to the physical appearance, the fortune, profession or education of those you meet, but to their soul and spirit, otherwise you will never know their essence. You can be sure that those who go about in this world in the guise of beggars and drunkards are really, in the eyes of God who created them, princes and princesses.

86. *Love without danger to others*

When you love someone, instead of clinging to him selfishly, think of linking him to Heaven, to the inexhaustible Fountainhead of life, so that he may constantly drink at that Source and be regenerated. Nothing is more important than to know how to love. If you want the one you love to be happy and fulfilled, try not to think of yourself too much, otherwise you will drag him into the lower regions of your own desires and lusts. To love someone is not to attach them to oneself ; on the contrary, it is to try to transcend oneself in the desire to do something magnificent for them, and there is nothing more magnificent than to link them to the Source.

Approach the one you love, look at her — or him — take her in your arms and raise her towards Heaven, link her with the Divine Mother or with Christ, the Heavenly Father or the Holy Spirit. If your relationship is not sufficiently intimate for you to take your beloved in your arms, you can still try to link her, by your thoughts, to the Source of light Wish her a true understanding of the new life ; wish her peace such as she has never known.

Let your love be such that it always contributes to the fulfilment of those you love.

87. *Love without danger to yourself*

Love is a force that works at making you resemble the one you love. If you love someone who is selfish, vulgar, dishonest and spiteful, his faults will eventually work their way into you and you will end by resembling him. But if you concentrate on the Lord, if you love Him, aware that He is immensity, that He is a boundless ocean of light and life, little by little, your consciousness will expand and become more luminous, and divine life will begin to flow within you. Know who to love, therefore. You can, of course, love all human beings — in fact you must do so — but, in order to avoid being contaminated and dragged down by their weaknesses, first and foremost you must love the Lord. He who loves the Lord can love anyone he pleases without risk to himself ; divine love will make him strong and keep him from danger.

When a life-guard dives into the water to save a drowning man, he lets him hang on to his feet, but if the man struggles and tries to clutch his arms, his rescuer has to knock him out, otherwise he would be dragged under and drown with him. And you must do the same : keep your arms for God and let human beings have your feet. Don't give them every scrap of your love, otherwise you will go under and drown with them. So many people love without any discrimination as to who, when and how they should love, and then they say that love is the cause of all unhappiness. What utter nonsense ! It is their ignorance about love that makes them unhappy, not love itself, for love is God, and God cannot be the cause of anything bad. You must begin by loving God and steeping yourself in His vibrations, then you will be able to love and help others without danger. Since you will be connected to the Source, you can pour your strength out on others without weakening yourself, for your supply of water will be continually renewed. But if you cut off the connection, you will soon dry up, for your own reserves cannot last for ever.

88. *You can only help others if you go to God for what they need*

Never abandon Heaven for anyone, not even for your child, not even for your husband or wife, for you can do them good only by remaining in contact with Heaven. You will ask, 'But what's wrong with devoting my time to my work or to my wife and children and friends ?' Nothing at all ; it is good to be conscientious and devoted and to do one's duty, but not to the point of neglecting Heaven. Sentimentality and blind attachment will get you nowhere.

What does a man do if he truly loves his family and sees that they are in need ? He has the courage to leave them, for a time, and go to a foreign country to earn some money, whereas someone who does not love his family so unselfishly will not have the courage to leave them. To all appearances, the first man abandons his family, but he does so in order to help them : he goes abroad and amasses a fortune and, when he comes home again, the whole family rejoices. But the man who does not have the courage to leave his family condemns both them and himself to lasting poverty.

Now, let's translate that : someone who truly loves his husband or wife, his children or his friends, is capable of abandoning them, from time to time, to go 'abroad', that is to say, to the divine world, where he amasses a fortune, and then, when he returns, he has presents for all of them. Whereas he who has not understood this stays with his family, but what will he have to give them ? Nothing but a few odds and ends, a few stale crusts. And how long should one stay 'abroad'. That depends ; it can be for half-an-hour or an hour, or a day …The only genuine love is that which gives others the purest treasures of Heaven.

89. *The circulation of love*

Don't be concerned about whether the person you love is also the one who loves you. Why not ? Because love circulates and flows from one to another ; it is something that we receive and that we must give. The person to whom you give your love will hand it on to the one he loves, and he to another and so on, thus forming a chain, a current that goes out from you and comes back to you again after flowing through thousands of other beings.

It is easy to understand this idea if you imagine that we are a team of mountaineers roped together for an ascent. Each member of the team must keep climbing and not allow the rope to go slack. If you say to the climber ahead of you, 'I love you ; turn round and look at me', you will be hindering the ascent of the whole team. To turn round would be to retreat, to let the rope go slack, to prevent those in front and behind from continuing the climb. Every individual must go in one direction only, in the direction of the ascent of the whole team. We have no business to stop to talk and look at each other ; we have to keep climbing, without faltering, towards the summit.

90. *Love is its own reward*

Our hearts must be full of love for human beings, because they are all our brothers and sisters.

We must think of them and help them without expecting the slightest reward, for, in reality, our reward is already given to us in that inner sense of expansion, that extraordinary sensation of warmth that fills us when we love. This is a marvellous reward ; life contains none greater.

Do you always expect to be rewarded for what you do ? If so, it shows how little you understand things. He who has understood the secret of love asks for nothing : he gives freely. And, because he radiates the climate of fulfilment and joy in which he lives, he wins the trust of quantities of friends. What better reward could you hope to find ?

91. *If you know how to open yourself to others you will never be lonely*

So many men and women complain of being lonely ! In spite of all the people around them, they still feel alone. In actual fact, it is their attitude that isolates them : they don't know how to open themselves to others ; they don't know how to love ; they don't know how to say even one little word of encouragement or consolation, and they don't know how to give. They always wait for others to come to them but others are often very busy ; they have their own worries and concerns. So, there they are, endlessly bewailing the fact that no one ever goes to see them, no one loves them, no one is interested in them. But why should it always be up to others to love and take an interest in them ? If you are unhappy because you are lonely, don't just sit there and do nothing about it. Instead of moping in a corner and waiting for some love and attention from others, take the initiative, go out to them. There is no reason to feel alone when love and light are there. If you feel lonely it is because you have shut yourself out from that love and light.

How often I have insisted on this : that you must stop being quite so egocentric and do something for others. Of course, it is often the education you received that is at fault. Parents tell their children, 'Don't be so stupid ; don't always be the one to make the first move ; let others come to you'. To be sure, others will come to them, but only if they know how to be useful. If you are a baker, people will come to you for bread. If you want people to come to you, you must be capable of giving something. A person who has nothing to give will never attract anyone, so he will always be alone. There is nothing to be gained by blaming others for not coming to you ; make yourself agreeable and they will soon start coming. Look at a newly-opened rose : everyone is attracted by its delicious scent, even bees and butterflies. Yes, because it has opened its petals. So, why keep your petals closed ? Why refuse to give off any perfume ?

92. *Only the presence of God can fill the void in the soul of man*

Everyone dreams of finding a being by whose side he may go forward, with confidence, on the path of life, a being with whom he can exchange his most intimate thoughts and emotions. But this is difficult. Innumerable novels, films and plays have been written in which men and women describe the anguish, the distress caused by the impossibility of finding such a being. And this impossibility comes from the fact that the human soul can be completely and finally fulfilled only by God Himself. He who wishes to conquer loneliness and feel himself filled with an immense presence of joy and happiness every day, must unite himself to God.

Solitude is a state of consciousness which even the greatest Initiates have experienced. Jesus himself cried out, 'My God, my God, why have You forsaken me ?' when he passed through this obscure, barren land. Every human being will experience this terrible solitude one day. Why ? Because one cannot really grow in faith, hope and love when one is happy and contented and surrounded by friends ; only when one is inwardly alone and abandoned. The only way to survive solitude is to lean on the Supreme Being who holds all worlds in His hand. We have to believe in that immortal Being, love Him and place all our hope in Him.

93. *Crossing the desert*

In the course of our spiritual life, it can happen that we feel as though we were in the middle of a parched, barren desert ; nothing appeals to us any more ; everything seems insipid and alien. This is the worst possible state for a spiritualist[3]. There is something worse than falling ill, losing all your money or experiencing failure, and it is to lose all spiritual impetus and feel that you no longer love or believe in anything. And, as this can happen to all of you, you must know how to deal with it.

Even in the aridity of the desert, you should be able to say, 'Lord God, I am in your hands ; this is the path You have led me to and, even without water, I'm going to stick to it. I am at your service, Lord ; help me, for I love You.' That's all. You must not relinquish your faith and love so easily ; on the contrary, your only hope of salvation is to advance with even greater ardour and twice as much faith. Don't let this impression of being lost in the middle of a desert blind you to everything else ; do everything in your power to press forward ; you are bound to find some fruit or some water, eventually, with which to slake your thirst. Even in the

3 The word 'spiritualist', in the language of Omraam Mikhaël Aïvanhov, simply means one who looks at things from a spiritual point of view, whose philosophy of life is based on belief in a spiritual reality.

middle of the desert there are oases. Keep going forward, therefore, until you find an oasis within you from which to drink, for the water that it contains is the water of humility and love, and it is this that will give you the strength to go on.

94. Purity allows us to be in contact with the divine world

You often complain that Heaven is deaf and cruel and never answers your prayers. The truth is that your whole being is immersed in the divine world and, if you feel isolated, if you feel a gulf between Heaven and yourself, it is because your inferior thoughts and feelings have built up layers of opaque matter that come between you and Heaven and prevent you from communicating with it. If you decide to work to purify yourself and make your subtle bodies more receptive and sensitive, you will see that, in fact, there is no gulf between you and Heaven.

It is very important for a spiritualist to know how to eliminate impurities from his psychic body. This is why exercises of purification must have a large place in his life, not only physical methods such as breathing exercises, ablutions, fasting, etc. but, also, the spiritual methods of concentration and prayer. By means of these exercises, he introduces into himself a substance which is capable of

disintegrating all harmful, alien elements and releas-
ing the flow of divine life in him once again. This
is why you must never forget to cleanse and purify
yourselves every day — in fact, not once but several
times a day. Let streams of pure water from Heaven
flow through you, and this purity will not only bring
you every blessing, but your presence will also be
beneficial to others : you will do good to all those
you meet, they will receive light from you and you
will be a means of putting them in contact with
Heaven.

95. *Heaven responds only to signals of light*

If you want to attract celestial spirits and give
them the desire to help you, you must live in accordance with the divine laws. Otherwise, they will
close their eyes and ears to you ; they will neither
see nor hear you, and you will be left to stumble
along in the dark. Only by the way you live can you
oblige them to pay attention to you. They have to
see a signal, a glimmer of light coming from you.
When celestial entities see a human being, afar off,
who projects brilliant flashes of light and colour
from his heart and soul and spirit, they say to each
other, 'Oh, look at the celebration going on down
there. Let's go and join in !' Then, they come to
him and become his friends ; often, in fact, they
decide to dwell in him permanently so as to help

him, and then everything becomes easier for him. This is why it is well worth improving the way you live because, in that way, you will win the support and even the permanent presence of these spirits of light who come to help you in your spiritual work.

96. Gratitude : the key to happiness

You come to me and complain, 'Oh, how unhappy I am !' 'I see that, but have you said 'thank you', today ?' 'Thank you ? Who should I thank and what have I got to be thankful for ?' 'Well, can you walk and breathe ?' 'Yes.' 'And did you have breakfast this morning ?' 'Yes.' 'And you can open your mouth to talk ?' 'Yes, again !' 'In that case, you should be grateful to God, because there are people who can neither walk nor eat nor open their mouths.'

You are unhappy because it never occurs to you to be grateful. If you want all that to change, you must begin by recognizing that nothing is more wonderful than the fact that you are alive and capable of moving about and seeing and talking. Do you have any idea how many billions and billions of elements and particles are involved simply in keeping a human being alive ? You never think of this, so you are always dissatisfied and resentful. Be grateful ! Tomorrow morning, as soon as you get up, give thanks to Heaven. So many men and women will never wake up again, or will wake up paralyzed. Think of that and say, 'Thank you, Lord ; You have given me life and health today ; I promise to do your will'.

Your gifts, talents and virtues are, in reality, envoys from Heaven, who have made their dwelling in you in order to work through you. You should be aware of this, for the day you begin to be too self-satisfied and proud of your success, as though all the merit belonged to you, these friends will fade away and you will lose that talent or virtue. So many people have lost a talent through pride ! And others, on the contrary, have won and amplified their qualities thanks to their humility.

And when, for no particular reason, you suddenly feel very happy and elated, it is because you have been visited by celestial entities. If you fail to appreciate what they do for you, you will lose that joyful state and, in spite of all your efforts to recapture it, it will never come back. It will be all over : those entities will never come to you again ; they will never look at you or smile or say a word to you again ; they will never make the slightest gesture towards you again. The one thing that offends the spirits of light is ingratitude. They want you to appreciate their love and generosity. They are not worried about your faults and failings ; in fact, they know all about them and even find excuses for you, saying, 'They're in such a sorry state, poor creatures ; we must do something to help them !' But, if they see that you don't appreciate their presence, they leave you alone. It is not that they need your gratitude for themselves, but they know that if you don't appreciate them, you will be incapable of benefiting from all that they can give you. Never forget, therefore : the greatest secret, the most important key to your happiness and progress is gratitude. As long as you appreciate all that Heaven gives you, it will never abandon you.

97. Learn to avoid evil

Suppose you go for a walk in a forest and lose your way. You have left the main road and followed a path which leads to a swampy area infested by flies, wasps, mosquitoes and snakes, and now you are being threatened and attacked and stung. What should you have done to avoid being stung ? You should have fled, turned round and gone back to the main road as soon as you saw where you were. How else can you avoid being attacked by all those creatures ? The only way is to leave their territory. Similarly, if you lose your way carelessly and wander onto the lower astral plane, the malicious entities that inhabit these regions will try to bite and sting you and you must get away from their territory in a hurry.

It is always unwise to remain within reach of negative currents on the psychic plane of thoughts, emotions and feelings, because you will be in danger of falling into their power ; it is much better to avoid the confrontation altogether. If you remain in darkness for too long, you will not conquer it ; it is the darkness that will conquer you. If you remain in a climate of hatred for too long, it will destroy you. If you remain in the grip of fear, sensuality, passion or viciousness for too long, it is they that will be victorious, not you. You must get away from them at once.

In this respect, the physical and psychic planes are not governed by the same laws : on the physical plane you must not give in if you are attacked ; you must resist with courage, will-power and tenacity. Your strength increases if you keep struggling. On the psychic plane, however, it is better not to confront hostile forces head on. You will ask, 'In that case, how can we avoid falling into their power ?' There are many, many ways, and one of the most effective is prayer.

98. Prayer : our safest haven

Prayer is the act by which we raise ourselves to the luminous world in which the Lord has placed everything we could possibly need in order to be healthy, fulfilled and at peace. The Lord Himself may not know when we need something and, in fact, it does not matter whether He knows or not, since all the elements our heart and soul desire are there, ready and waiting for us. It is up to us to go and get them and, if need be, take refuge there.

Let me illustrate this : you are being pursued by enemies and you are running as fast as you can to get away from them. At last, panting and dusty, you find yourself amongst a throng of people who are eating and drinking and making merry in the midst of songs, dances and perfumes. No one says, 'Hey, you there ! What do you think you're doing ? Get out ; you were not invited !' On the contrary, they make you welcome, give you what you need to wash and change your clothes and urge you to join them at the banquet. Your enemies, in the meantime, are cooling their heels outside ; they are powerless to hurt you. Well, that is what prayer is : you run away as hard as you can — that is to say, you escape from the harmful currents and malicious entities that are persecuting you — and reach the place where the Lord is rejoicing in the midst of the Angels, Archangels and all the divinities of Heaven. He asks nothing better than to welcome you in their midst and you may stay as long as you like, while your enemies retreat in confusion. Later, you will go home, happy and contented.

From now on, therefore, when you are tormented and distressed, instead of moping and

moaning and telling everyone your troubles or having recourse to tranquilizers or stimulants, try to
rise to another region by means of prayer, this most
marvellous and effective method bequeathed to us
by the greatest Masters of mankind. Remember,
when the situation is very bad, that it won't last for
ever and that all you have to do is go away. Yes :
move away. The Lord will not come and look for
you where you are ; it is not up to Him to get you
out of Hell and take you to Heaven, it is up to you
to make the effort to climb up to Him.

99. Live your spiritual joys over again

When you manage to achieve a really desirable
state of mind, the question is, of course, how to
make it last. The thing to know is that, once you
have experienced a state of real harmony and fulfilment, it is as though it were engraved within you
and that engraving is always there, it cannot be eras-
ed. 'In that case' you will say, 'Why doesn't that
state last ? Why do I feel discouraged and anxious
almost immediately ?' Because life is a perpetual
outpouring : the seconds go by, offering you an
endless succession of new impressions and new
events and, as you are not sufficiently vigilant, you
are unable to stay with the same impressions. You
let yourself be carried away by other ideas, other
sentiments or activities, and so you lose your peace

and joy. But there is one thing you can be sure of, and that is that the impressions you have experienced are still there, inside you, tidily filed away like the discs or tapes in your record library. One day, when you remember that you have a recording of a glorious voice singing celestial songs, you can get out the disc and put it on your inner record-player, and there you are : under the spell of that voice, you have recaptured the same state. You must remember to do this, to put on these divine recordings and listen to them over and over again.

Of course, I know very well that you are often worried and harassed in your lives but, believe me, it is always possible to recapture, sustain and store up these higher states of consciousness. You simply have to get into the habit of being constantly vigilant, constantly aware of the divine world and, starting first thing in the morning, go through all the ordinary gestures and activities of your everyday lives with your thoughts turned towards Heaven.

If you get into the habit of maintaining this attitude throughout the day, you will see that nothing disturbs you for long. To be sure, we shall always be upset by certain events — some bad news, an illness or an accident — I don't deny it. But if you have acquired the habit of holding on to those higher states, you will get over these vicissitudes much sooner, because you will have understood that God has given omnipotence to the spirit, not to matter.

Treasure every instant in which you have experienced a divine state of consciousness for as long as possible, therefore, for every one of those instants is eternal ; you can always recapture it, for it is engraved within you and nobody can take it from you.

100. *Be loyal to your principles*

You must associate with other human beings, live with them, love them and help them, but you must be careful not to share their weaknesses. Give them some particles, some rays from your heart and soul, but without losing anything of your ideal, that is to say, without making concessions or compromising your spiritual principles. Whatever happens, you must remain honest, upright and truthful and hold staunchly and unwaveringly to your convictions while, at the same time, being flexible with other people.

Even if he is chopped up in little bits, a true servant of God remains unshakeable in his faith and love. But to achieve this, he has to possess the teachings of Initiatic Science. Anyone who imagines that, without this knowledge, he can plunge into the maelstrom of life and emerge intact, is deluding

himself. There are so many things that can beguile
you, lead you astray and destroy your equilibrium.
If you overestimate your strength, you will go under,
like all the others. So, study, develop your will-
power and, above all, make an effort to keep alive
within you all the truths of the Teaching. Tell
yourself, 'I know that I can never escape from the
realities of everyday life, but I must be on my
guard ; come what may, I will allow nothing to
make me lose the flame of enthusiasm and hope.'
Hold on to these truths ; by means of meditation
and prayer, fill your lungs with oxygen, and then
go and face up to reality. If you do this, then,
indeed, you will become truly strong and powerful.

101. Recognize whether a person's influence on you is good or bad

Suppose that you see a great deal of a certain
person and you are not sure that it is good for you
to be with him so much. It is very easy to find out :
if you feel that he stimulates you to be more lucid,
generous and kind, if he encourages you in your
work, continue to associate with him. Whatever
other people may say about him, he does you good
and that is what matters. But if, on the contrary,
you realize that when you see him, your ideas are
less clear, that you don't know whether you are
coming or going, that you feel only animosity and

disgust for others and that you have no enthusiasm to undertake anything, then you must try not to see him any more. Even if he is a celebrity, a multi-millionaire, wash your hands of him, because he has a very bad influence on you.

102. Open yourself to good influences

When you are seized with delight and admiration at the sight of a flower, you immediately sense that that flower is a presence that speaks to you by its form, colours and scent. And this presence slips into you, through your subtle bodies, and awakens the forms, colours and perfumes that correspond to it in your soul. The same can be true, of course, of something repulsive : you feel it as a presence that introduces noxious elements into you. Everything around you influences you, whether you are aware of it or not. And the important thing is precisely this : to become aware of it so as to be on your guard and expose yourself, insofar as that is possible, only to good influences. As soon as you sense that a human being or an object has a good influence on you, you must consciously open your inner doors and allow that influence to penetrate the depths of your being. If you don't open yourself, even the very best influences will be ineffectual ; they will not touch you.

Go and stand by a stream or a spring of water and meditate on the image it gives you of the true source of life which must flow within you. Go to the sun, contemplate it, open yourself to it, so that it may awaken within you the spiritual sun, with all its warmth and light. Go to the flowers and ask them for the secret of their fragrance. Listen carefully and learn from them how to extract the most fragrant quintessences from your own heart and soul. If you are careful to open yourself only to influences that are pure, beautiful and harmonious, you, yourself, will become a blessing for all those who approach you.

103. The influence of works of art

Everything that a human being sees and hears affects his nervous system and, if so many people today show signs of being psychically disturbed, it is because, more and more, they are living in the midst of ugliness and disorder. Even art, which should be their link with the world of beauty and harmony, has ceased to fulfil its mission. More and more, poetry is simply a string of words which each person interprets in his own way ; music consists of weird noises and violent, chaotic rhythms, and painting is a jumble of meaningless lines and colours thrown haphazardly onto canvas. And the effect of all this on human beings is extremely negative, because it makes them revert to chaos.

Show discrimination, therefore, in choosing the books you read, the music you listen to and the pictures and shows you look at. Try to pay attention only to the creations of artists who are truly inspired by Heaven. In this way, you will have a link with those who are more advanced than yourself and will begin to sense and experience something of what these creators experienced and, almost in spite of yourself, you will be obliged to follow in their footsteps. They will lead you to the regions that they themselves contemplated and explored and in those regions you, too, will taste true life.

104. Use objects consciously and with love

Think of all the tools, utensils and objects of all kinds that you use every day ! Most of the time you handle them absent-mindedly or even roughly and clumsily. Why don't you use them consciously and lovingly ? Even if you cannot accept the notion that the way you handle things can be either beneficial or harmful for them, you will certainly have to admit that it affects you. Experiment with this and you will see that the effect on you is different when you handle things roughly and when you handle them with love. Whatever we do, whatever gesture we make, we must learn to put something better, something more spiritual into it.

105. Consecrate places and objects

You all have a house or a flat — or, at least, a room — in which you live, and you all use a certain number of objects every day. You must consecrate these objects and the place in which you live, and dedicate them to the Deity, so that they may be used only in the service of good. Ask Heaven to send luminous spirits to help you to rid them of all negative particles and influences, then dedicate them to a virtue or a Heavenly entity. Ask that entity to dwell in your home or to impregnate these objects so as to have a good influence on you and your family, on the health as well as on the intellect, soul and spirit of your husband or wife and children. Get into the habit of doing this and you will see how much it helps and supports and strengthens you.

106. We leave our imprints wherever we go

Every single thing we do in the course of the day leaves permanent traces, imprints that are stamped into the memory of the etheric world and cling to the walls, the furniture and the objects in all the places we have been in. It is not necessary to touch something in order to leave traces on it ; even if you don't touch anything, your mere presence and the emanations of your physical, astral and mental bodies is enough to leave your imprint, and the places you have been in as well as the people you have associated with bear the mark, good or bad, luminous or dark, of your presence. This is why it is so important to work to improve and purify your thoughts and feelings, knowing that it is not only through your acts but, also, through your thoughts and feelings that you do good or evil.

Wherever you go and whatever you do, try to leave traces only of light and love. If you are walking down a country lane or a city street, bless that lane or that street and pray that all those who come after you may receive peace and light, that they may be led on the right path, that they may vibrate in unison with the divine world.

107. Our influence on human beings and on the whole of creation

Human beings rarely pay attention to the positive or negative effect their own state of mind has on others. Even with those they love they are careless and unthinking. In fact, it is when a man is feeling melancholy and out of sorts that he consoles himself by going to embrace his sweetheart without knowing or caring that, with every kiss, he is giving her his own woes and his own despondency. And a great many parents do the same with their children. In their exchanges, men and women are continually giving each other something, but the Lord only knows — or perhaps it is the Devil who knows — what it is that they give and receive !

Never touch someone else, particularly a child, when you are tense and angry or upset, and never give them anything, either, because your anger and tension will have a negative influence on them. Also, when you have to prepare a meal, take care not to do so in a negative frame of mind, because your thoughts and feelings are absorbed by the food that your family or friends are going to eat. Learn to pay attention to everything you do and to develop your consciousness and your sensitivity.

You must never lose sight of the fact that you are not the only one to be affected by your inner state : it also influences others. Even if you don't feel this very distinctly, you are linked to every member of your family and of society and, when you make progress, all the treasures and light that you receive reflect on every single one of them. When you advance, they advance, too. They may not see this any more than you do, but Heaven sees that their progress is due to you. And the same is true if you deteriorate and start to go downhill : your family and the whole of society, because of the bond between you, is influenced negatively.

Thus, we all carry others along with us, either to Heaven or to Hell : we are all responsible for each other.

Now, do you want to be useful and to help all mankind and even the animals, plants and trees ? If so, try to make your life more and more spiritual. In this way, subtly and imperceptibly, you will be carrying the whole of creation upwards ; you will be drawing down blessings on all human beings.

108. We are free to accept or reject influences

You must realize that it always depends on you whether you accept a particular influence or not. Even the spirits of evil have no power over you if you shut your doors to them. Of course, if you are without discernment, if you don't know how to protect yourself or what precautions to take, they can drag you down to Hell. They know what they have to do and the different kinds of bait to use to tempt you and, if you yield, if you swallow their bait, you will be caught in their net and, very gently, very gradually, they will drag you down to your death. God has given them this power, but only if you are weak and unenlightened. If you place yourself under the influence of the spirits of light and refuse to let the spirits of evil lure you into their snares, you will be beyond their reach and they will have no power over you.

109. Purify yourself
of all that nourishes undesirable entities

If you leave scraps of food lying about in your house, all kinds of insects and vermin — flies, wasps, ants, mice, etc. — will arrive and start feeding on it. Dirt and rubbish attract them. If you want to get rid of them, you will have to clean up, otherwise they will always be there. To kill them or drive them away will never rid you of them entirely as long as you leave the rubbish lying about, for there will always be others to take their place. The only way to get rid of them for good is to clean your house, for then they will go and look for food elsewhere. Similarly, you must realize that, if you entertain certain bad, impure feelings, thoughts or desires, they will attract 'vermin' from the world of darkness that love to feed on such impurities, and you will be plagued and tormented by them. Try as you might, as long as you harbour elements within you that rot and ferment, you will be a prey to these undesirable entities. If you want to get rid of them, you must be careful about your thoughts and feelings and work to purify them and transform them into a delicious nourishment for Heavenly spirits.

110. Consecrate yourself to the spirits of light

The space around us is inhabited by billions of malignant entities who have sworn to destroy the human race. To be sure, it is also inhabited by countless luminous entities who are there to help and protect us, but the help and protection they offer can never be truly effective if human beings do nothing to help themselves.

If your heart and soul and spirit remain open to the four winds without being consecrated and surrounded by a barrier of light, spirits of darkness and all kinds of undesirable entities have the right to enter you, work their mischief and go off with all your treasures. It is not they that are to blame ; it is up to you to do whatever needs to be done to keep them out and attract, instead, spirits of light. Call on the spirits of light, every day, saying, 'Lord God, Divine Mother, Most Holy Trinity, all you Angels and Archangels, servants of God and of the light, my Heavenly friends, my whole being belongs to you ! Make your dwelling within me, make use of me, do with me what you will for the glory of God and the coming of His Kingdom on earth'. Make this your prayer, every day, otherwise, you need not be surprised if you are invaded by beings of a very different kind.

If you do not think of inviting Heavenly entities to dwell in you, you must expect others, not at all Heavenly, to come and take up residence within you. It is up to you to decide who your 'tenants' will be. If you don't invite Angels, they won't try to occupy you, because they respect your freedom.

But devils will enter you without waiting for an invitation, for they respect nothing. It is up to you to decide if you want Angels and to say the magic words of invitation : 'Behold, this is my home ; I am the master here and I invite you to come and make use of all I have ; it is yours.' When the spirits of light sense that that is what the owner wants they have no hesitation in attacking and driving out any intruders. But, as long as the owner of the house does not call on them, they will do nothing, because they respect his free will. These are the divine rules.

111. Win the protection of Heaven by putting yourself at its service

If you are in the service of the government, you are under the protection of the State and, in theory, if someone attacks you, your rights will be defended by the State which watches over your interests. Similarly, he who becomes the servant of Heaven and begins to work for the divine cause acquires the same privileges and the invisible world watches over his interests. The Angels protect and take care of him and he no longer feels that he is all alone in life's wilderness, for he is a member of the immense divine family. If you put yourself at the service of Heaven and contribute to the establishment of the Kingdom of God and His Righteousness on earth, your life will be shielded by a powerful canopy of protection, and luminous entities will be always at your side to support and enlighten you.

112. A truly potent talisman

During the war, people would stick strips of paper on their windows to prevent them from being shattered by the blast when the bombs fell : the strips of paper neutralized the vibrations of the explosion. You can usefully transpose this phenomenon onto the level of your inner life : it can happen that you are 'bombarded' by evil thoughts and feelings and your 'windows' are in danger of being shattered. When this happens, you can protect yourself by sticking strips of paper on your windows. In other words, if you cherish the image of a saint, of a prophet or of Christ in your heart and concentrate on it, the strength of your love and veneration will counteract the bad vibrations and enable you to resist them.

Christianity has always had its mystics who contemplated and adored the face of Christ and considered it a strong talisman capable of enlightening them and protecting them from evil. If you really want to possess a talisman, choose the face of a pure, luminous, just and wise being, a true son or daughter of God, and contemplate it at length, every day, making an effort to identify with it.

113. The aura : our best protection

Human beings have perfected all kinds of devices for their protection and defence on the physical plane, things such as safes, locks and bolts, steel doors, burglar alarms, etc., not to mention all the different kinds of weapons : cannons, tanks, rockets and missiles, etc. On the spiritual level, however, in spite of all the tools and weapons that exist, they are still poor, defenceless and vulnerable. And yet, everything that is invented on the physical level has its equivalent on the spiritual level. The physical garments, for instance, that protect us from heat and cold, wind and rain, sharp objects and the sting of insects, have their equivalent on the spiritual plane in the aura, which is one of the most effective forms of protection we have.

Man's true garment is his aura which contains all the colours that represent his qualities and virtues. The aura is the spiritual robe that our virtues, particularly our qualities of purity and inner light, weave around us and, when we wear this garment, undesirable entities who find no nourishment in it and who cannot bear the light, have nothing more to hang on to, so they leave us. The aura has a magical function : it influences the spirits of the invisible world, attracting the entities of light and repulsing entities of darkness. Every day you should

think of forming a circle of light around you and
imagining, at the centre of this circle, an ever-
flowing source of light whose beneficial waves
stream over you and all around you.

114. The Lord is our centre of gravity

If you succeed in placing the Lord at the
forefront of your existence, above all your desires
and personal interests, a tremendous process of
transformation will take place within you and you
will become an organized world. To place the Lord
at the crowning point of our being is to anchor
ourselves to an indestructible centre of gravity.
When a physical object is firmly attached to its
centre of gravity, it can be pushed and pulled in all
directions but it will automatically regain its balance,
and the same is true of a human being. Unless and
until you have found a stable centre of gravity in
God, you will be knocked off balance by every little upheaval in your life. But, once you manage to
put all your hope and faith, all your love and trust
in your Creator, whatever comes, you will always
remain firm and invulnerable.

115. Consecrate your heart to God

You can never be completely safe unless you give
everything to God : spirit, soul and body. In fact,

you must also give Him your house and all your money, because the Lord is the only one who can tell you how to use these things in the service of good. But, above and beyond everything else, it is your heart that God asks of you. Why ? Because it is through your heart that the Evil One can enter you. The heart corresponds to the astral plane and the astral plane borders on the physical plane and is, consequently, more easily influenced by the dark forces of the underworld than the mind or soul or, especially, the spirit. However much evil you do, the spirit cannot be persuaded to do wrong ; the spirit is a spark that cannot be dimmed or extinguished, for it is too close to God.

The Lord asks for your heart, and you reply, 'Why do you want my heart, Lord ? I've given it to So-and-so'. 'That's all right', says the Lord, 'I know that. But give it to me, all the same, because all your misfortunes and griefs come from the fact that you keep your heart for yourself and that it can only lead you astray'.

Give your heart to God, then it will always be safe. He, at least, knows how to hold it without dropping it, whereas you can never be sure that, if you give it to someone else, they won't drop it. As long as you have not consecrated your heart to the Lord, you will continue to be exposed to serious problems in your inner life. So many exceptional beings have allowed their hearts to lead them into every kind of disorder and folly ! Ah, the heart ! No human being is proof against the demons who seek to get hold of his heart. This is why you must always seek the protection of Heaven by giving your heart to God. If you do this, God will send Angels to dwell in it and keep it safe.

INDEX

D ————————

F _____

G _____

H _____

I _____

P _____

S _____

T _____

By the same author:

Izvor Collection

201 - Toward a Solar Civilization
It is not enough to be familiar with the astronomical theory of heliocentricity. Since the sun is the centre of our universe, we must learn to put it at the centre of all our preoccupations and activities.

202 - Man, Master of His Destiny
If human beings are to be masters of their own destiny, they must understand that the laws which govern their physical, psychic and spiritual life are akin to those which govern the universe.

203 - Education Begins Before Birth
Humanity will improve and be transformed only when people realize the true import of the act of conception. In this respect, men and women have a tremendous responsibility for which they need years of preparation.

204 - The Yoga of Nutrition
The way we eat is as important as what we eat. Through our thoughts and feelings, it is possible to extract from our food spiritual elements which can contribute to the full flowering of our being.

205 - Sexual Force or the Winged Dragon
How to master, domesticate and give direction to our sexual energy so as to soar to the highest spheres of the spirit.

206 - A Philosophy of Universality
We must learn to replace our restricted, self-centred point of view with one that is immensely broad and universal. If we do this we shall all benefit; not only materially but particularly on the level of consciousness.

207 - What is a Spiritual Master
A true spiritual Master is, first, one who is conscious of the essential truths written by cosmic intelligence into the great book of Nature. Secondly, he must have achieved complete mastery of the elements of his own being. Finally, all the knowledge and authority he has acquired must serve only to manifest the qualities and virtues of selfless love.

208 - Under the Dove, the Reign of Peace
Peace will finally reign in the world only when human beings work to establish peace within themselves, in their every thought, feeling and action.

209 - Christmas and Easter in the Initiatic Tradition

Human beings are an integral part of the cosmos and intimately concerned by the process of gestation and birth going on in nature. Christmas and Easter – rebirth and resurrection – are simply two ways of envisaging humanity's regeneration and entry into the spiritual life.

210 - The Tree of the Knowledge of Good and Evil

Methods, not explanations, are the only valid answers to the problem of evil. Evil is an inner and outer reality which confronts us every day, and we must learn to deal with it.

211 - Freedom, the Spirit Triumphant

A human being is a spirit, a spark sprung from within the Almighty. Once a person understands, sees and feels this truth, he will be free.

212 - Light is a Living Spirit

Light, the living matter of the universe, is protection, nourishment and an agency for knowledge for human beings. Above all, it is the only truly effective means of self-transformation.

213 - Man's Two Natures, Human and Divine

Man is that ambiguous creature that evolution has placed on the borderline between the animal world and the divine world. His nature is ambivalent, and it is this ambivalence that he must understand and overcome.

214 - Hope for the World: Spiritual Galvanoplasty

On every level of the universe, the masculine and feminine principles reproduce the activity of those two great cosmic principles known as the Heavenly Father and the Divine Mother of which every manifestation of nature and life are a reflection. Spiritual galvanoplasty is a way of applying the science of these two fundamental principles to one's inner life.

215 - The True Meaning of Christ's Teaching

Jesus incorporated into the Our Father – or Lord's Prayer – an ancient body of knowledge handed down by Tradition and which had existed long before his time. A vast universe is revealed to one who knows how to interpret each of the requests formulated in this prayer.

216 - The Living Book of Nature

Everything in nature is alive and it is up to us to learn how to establish a conscious relationship with creation so as to receive that life within ourselves.

217 - New Light on the Gospels

The Parables and other tales from the Gospels are here interpreted as situations and events applicable to our own inner life.

218 - The Symbolic Language of Geometrical Figures

Each geometrical figure – circle, triangle, pentagram, pyramid or cross – is seen as a structure fundamental to the organization of the macrocosm (the universe) and the microcosm (human beings).

219 - Man's Subtle Bodies and Centres

However highly developed our sense organs, their scope will never reach beyond the physical plane. To experience richer and subtler sensations, human beings must exercise the subtler organs and spiritual centres that they also possess: the aura, the solar plexus, the Hara centre, the Chakras, and so on.

220 - The Zodiac, Key to Man and to the Universe

Those who are conscious of being part of the universe feel the need to work inwardly in order to find within themselves the fullness of the cosmic order so perfectly symbolized by the Zodiac.

221 - True Alchemy or The Quest for Perfection

Instead of fighting our weaknesses and vices – we would inevitably be defeated – we must learn to make them work for us. We think it normal to harness the untamed forces of nature, so why be surprised when a Master, an initiate, speaks of harnessing the primitive forces within us? This is true spiritual alchemy.

222 - Man's Psychic Life: Elements and Structures

"Know thyself" How to interpret this precept carved over the entrance to the temple at Delphi? To know oneself is to be conscious of one's different bodies, from the denser to the most subtle, of the principles which animate these bodies, of the needs they induce in one, and of the state of consciousness which corresponds to each.

223 - Creation: Artistic and Spiritual

Everyone needs to create but true creation involves spiritual elements. Artists, like those who seek the spirit, have to reach beyond themselves in order to receive elements from the higher planes.

224 - The Powers of Thought

Thought is a power, an instrument given to us by God so that we may become creators like himself – creators in beauty and perfection. This means that we must be extremely watchful, constantly verifying that what we do with our thoughts is truly for our own good and that of the whole world. This is the one thing that matters.

225 - Harmony and Health

Illness is a result of some physical or psychic disorder. The best defence against illness, therefore, is harmony. Day and night we must take care to be attuned and in harmony with life as a whole, with the boundless life of the cosmos.

226 - The Book of Divine Magic

True, divine magic, consists in never using the faculties, knowledge, or powers one has acquired for one's own self-interest, but always and only for the establishment of God's kingdom on earth.

227 - Golden Rules for Everyday Life

Why spoil one's life by chasing after things that matter less than life itself? Those who learn to give priority to life, who protect and preserve it in all integrity, will find more and more that they obtain their desires. For it is this, an enlightened, luminous life that can give them everything.

228 - Looking into the Invisible

Meditation, dreams, visions, astral projection all give us access to the invisible world, but the quality of the revelations received depends on our efforts to elevate and refine our perceptions.

229 - The Path of Silence

In every spiritual teaching, practices such as meditation and prayer have only one purpose: to lessen the importance attributed to one's lower nature and give one's divine nature more and more scope for expression. Only in this way can a human being experience true silence.

230 - The Book of Revelations: A Commentary

If *Revelations* is a difficult book to interpret it is because we try to identify the people, places and events it describes instead of concentrating on the essence of its message: a description of the elements and processes of our spiritual life in relation to the life of the cosmos.

231 - The Seeds of Happiness

Happiness is like a talent which has to be cultivated. Those who want to possess happiness must go in search of the elements which will enable them to nourish it inwardly; elements which belong to the divine world.

232 - The Mysteries of Fire and Water

Our psychic life is fashioned every day by the forces we allow to enter us, the influences that impregnate us. What could be more poetic, more meaningful than water and fire and the different forms under which they appear?

233 - Youth: Creators of the Future
Youth is full of life, enthusiasms and aspirations of every kind. The great question is how to channel its extraordinary, overflowing effervescence of energies.

234 - Truth, Fruit of Wisdom and Love
We all abide by our own "truth", and it is in the name of their personal "truth" that human beings are continually in conflict. Only those who possess true love and true wisdom discover the same truth and speak the same language.

235 - In Spirit and in Truth
Since we live on earth we are obliged to give material form to our religious beliefs. Sacred places and objects, rites, prayers and ceremonies are expressions of those beliefs. It is important to understand that they are no more than expressions – expressions which are always more or less inadequate. They are not themselves the religion, for religion exists in spirit and in truth.

236 - Angels and Other Mysteries of the Tree of Life
God is like a pure current of electricity which can reach us only through a series of transformers. These transformers are the countless luminous beings which inhabit the heavens and which tradition calls the Angelic Hierarchies. It is through them that we receive divine life; through them that we are in contact with God.

237 - Cosmic Balance, the Secret of Polarity
Libra – the Scales – symbolizes cosmic balance, the equilibrium of the two opposite and complementary forces, the masculine and feminine principles, by means of which the universe came into being and continues to exist. The symbolism of Libra, expression of this twofold polarity, dominates the whole of creation.

By the same author
(translated from the French)

"Complete Works" Collection

Volume 1 — The Second Birth
Volume 2 — Spiritual Alchemy
Volume 5 — Life Force
Volume 6 — Harmony
Volume 7 — The Mysteries of Yesod
Volume 10 — The Splendour of Tiphareth
                  The Yoga of the Sun
Volume 11 — The Key to the Problems of Existence
Volume 12 — Cosmic Moral Law
Volume 13 — A New Earth
                  Methods, Exercises, Formulas, Prayers
Volume 14 — Love and Sexuality (Part I)
Volume 15 — Love and Sexuality (Part II)
Volume 17 — 'Know Thyself' Jnana Yoga (Part I)
Volume 18 — 'Know Thyself' Jnana Yoga (Part II)
Volume 25 — A New Dawn: Society and Politics
                  in the Light of Initiatic Science (Part I)
Volume 26 — A New Dawn: Society and Politics
                  in the Light of Initiatic Science (Part II)
Volume 29 — On the Art of Teaching (Part III)
Volume 30 — Life and Work in an Initiatic School
                  Training for the Divine
Volume 32 — The Fruits of the Tree of Life
                  The Cabbalistic Tradition

Brochures:
New Presentation

301 — The New Year
302 — Meditation
303 — Respiration
304 — Death and the Life Beyond

Live Recordings on Tape

KC2510An — The Laws of Reincarnation
(Two audio cassettes)

(available in French only)

K 2001 Fr — La science de l'unité
K 2002 Fr — Le bonheur
K 2003 Fr — La vraie beauté
K 2004 Fr — L'éternel printemps
K 2005 Fr — La loi de l'enregistrement
K 2006 Fr — La science de l'éducation
K 2007 Fr — La prière
K 2008 Fr — L'esprit et la matière
K 2009 Fr — Le monde des archétypes
K 2010 Fr — L'importance de l'ambiance
K 2011 Fr — Le yoga de la nutrition
K 2012 Fr — L'aura
K 2013 Fr — Déterminisme et indéterminisme
K 2014 Fr — Les deux natures de l'être humain
K 2015 Fr — Prendre et donner
K 2016 Fr — La véritable vie spirituelle
K 2017 Fr — La mission de l'art
K 2018 Fr — Il faut laisser l'amour véritable se manifester
K 2019 Fr — Comment orienter la force sexuelle
K 2020 Fr — Un haut idéal pour la jeunesse
K 2021 Fr — La réincarnation - Preuves de la réincarnation
dans les Évangiles.
K 2022 Fr — La réincarnation - Rien ne se produit par hasard,
une intelligence préside à tout.
K 2023 Fr — La réincarnation - L'aura et la réincarnation.
K 2024 Fr — La loi de la responsabilité
K 2551 Fr — La réincarnation (coffret de 3 cassettes)
K 2552 Fr — Introduction à l'astrologie initiatique
(coffret de 3 cassettes)
K 2553 Fr — La méditation (coffret de 3 cassettes)

World Wide - Editor-Distributor
Editions PROSVETA S.A. - B.P. 12 - F - 83601 Fréjus Cedex (France)
Tel. (00 33) 04 94 40 82 41 - Fax (00 33) 04 94 40 80 05
Web: **www.prosveta.com**
E-mail: **international@prosveta.com**

Distributors

AUSTRALIA
SURYOMA LTD
P.O. Box 798 – Brookvale – N.S.W. 2100
Tel. / Fax: (61) 2 9984 8500 – E-mail: suryoma@csi.com

AUSTRIA
HARMONIEQUELL VERSAND – A-5302 Henndorf, Hof 37
Tel. / Fax: (43) 6214 7413 – E-mail: info@prosveta.at

BELGIUM
PROSVETA BENELUX – Liersesteenweg 154 B-2547 Lint
Tel.: (32) 3/455 41 75 – Fax: 3/454 24 25
N.V. MAKLU Somersstraat 13-15 – B-2000 Antwerpen
Tel.: (32) 3/321 29 00 – E-mail: prosveta@skynet.be
VANDER S.A. – Av. des Volontaires 321 – B-1150 Bruxelles
Tel.: (32) 27 62 98 04 – Fax: 27 62 06 62

BRAZIL
NOBEL SA – Rua da Balsa, 559 – CEP 02910 - São Paulo, SP

BULGARIA
SVETOGLED – Bd Saborny 16 A, appt 11 – 9000 Varna
E-mail: svetgled@revolta.com

CANADA
PROSVETA Inc. – 3950, Albert Mines – North Hatley, QC J0B 2C0
Tel.: (1) 819 564-8212 – Fax: (1) 819 564-1823
In Canada, call toll free: 1-800-854-8212
E-mail: prosveta@prosveta-canada.com — www.prosveta-canada.com

COLUMBIA
PROSVETA – Avenida 46 no 19-14 (Palermo) – Santafé de Bogotá
Tel.: (57) 232-01-36 – Fax: (57) 633-58-03

CYPRUS
THE SOLAR CIVILISATION BOOKSHOP
73 D Kallipoleos Avenue - Lycavitos – P.O. Box 4947, 1355 – Nicosia
Tel.: 02 377503 and 09 680854

CZECH REPUBLIC
PROSVETA Tchèque – Ant. Sovy 18 – České Budejovice 370 05
Tel. / Fax: 0042038-53 00 227 – E-mail: prosveta@seznam.cz

GERMANY
PROSVETA Deutschland – Postfach 16 52 – 78616 Rottweil
Tel.: (49) 741 46551 – Fax: (49) 741 46552 – E-mail: Prosveta.de@t-online.de
EDIS GmbH, Mühlweg 2 – 82054 Sauerlach
Tel.: (49) 8104-6677-0 – Fax: (49) 8104-6677-99

GREAT BRITAIN & IRELAND
PROSVETA – The Doves Nest, Duddleswell Uckfield – East Sussex TN 22 3JJ
Tel.: (44) (01825) 712988 – Fax: (44) (01825) 713386
E-mail: prosveta@pavilion.co.uk

Omraam Mikhaël Aivanhov

☐ I wish to be on your mailing list to receive free information on Prosveta's publications

☐ Please send me details of meetings and activities of the Universal White Brotherhood.

☐ I wish to support the work of Prosveta and enclose a donation herewith.

Book Distributors for the Universal White Brotherhood. Registered Charity No. 288339

Name (Please print) ....

Address ....

Town .... County ....

Postcode .... Tel: ....

PROSVETA

The Doves Nest
Duddleswell
Uckfield
TN22 3JJ

GREECE
PROSVETA – VAMVACAS INDUSTRIAL EQUIPEMENT
Moutsopoulou 103 – 18541 Piraeus
HAITI
B.P. 115 – Jacmel, Haiti (W.I .) – Tel. / Fax: (509) 288-3319
HOLLAND
STICHTING PROSVETA NEDERLAND
Zeestraat 50 – 2042 LC Zandvoort – E-mail: prosveta@worldonline.nl
HONG KONG
SWINDON BOOK CO LTD
246 Deck 2, Ocean Terminal – Harbour City – Tsimshatsui, Kowloon
ISRAEL
ÉDITIONS GALATAIA – 58 Bar-Kohva street – Tel Aviv
Tel.: 00 972 3 5286264 – Fax: 00 972 3 5286260
ITALY
PROSVETA Coop. – Casella Postale – 06060 Moiano (PG)
Tel. / Fax: (39) 075-8358498 – E-mail: prosveta@tin.it
LUXEMBOURG
PROSVETA BENELUX – Liersesteenweg 154 - B-2547 Lint
NORWAY
PROSVETA NORDEN – Postboks 5101 – 1503 Moss
Tel.: 69 26 51 40 – Fax: 69 25 06 76
E-mail: prosveta Norden – prosnor@online.no
PORTUGAL
PUBLICAÇÕES EUROPA-AMERICA Ltd
Est Lisboa-Sintra KM 14 – 2726 Mem Martins Codex
ROMANIA
ANTAR – Str. N. Constantinescu 10 – Bloc 16A - sc A - Apt. 9
Sector 1 – 71253 Bucarest
Tel.: (40) 1 679 52 48 – Tel. / Fax: (40) 1 231 37 19
RUSSIA
Neapolitensky – 40 Gorohovaya - Appt 1 – Saint-Petersbourg
Tel.: (70) 812 5327 184 / (70) 812 2726 876 – Fax: (70) 812 1582 363
SINGAPORE & MALAYSIA
AMERICASIA GLOBAL MARKETING – Clementi Central Post Office
P.O. Box 108 – Singapore 911204 – Tel.: (65) 892 0503 – Fax: (65) 95 199 198
E-mail: harvard1@mbox4.singnet.com.sg
SPAIN
ASOCIACIÓN PROSVETA ESPAÑOLA – C/ Ausias March nº 23 Ático
SP-08010 Barcelona — Tel.: (34) (3) 412 31 85 – Fax: (34) (3) 302 13 72
SWITZERLAND
PROSVETA Société Coopérative – CH - 1808 Les Monts-de-Corsier
Tel.: (41) 21 921 92 18 – Fax: (41) 21 922 92 04
E-mail: prosveta@swissonline.ch
UNITED STATES
PROSVETA U.S.A. – P.O. Box 1176 – New Smyrna Beach, FL.32170-1176
Tel. / Fax: (904) 428-1465
E-mail: sales@prosveta-usa .com — www.prosveta-usa.com
VENEZUELA
BETTY MUNÕZ – Urbanización Los Corales – avenida Principal
Quinta La Guarapa – LA GUAÏRA – Municipio Vargas

Printed by
Imprimerie H.L.N.
Sherbrooke (Quebec) Canada
in March 2000